Heirlooms

BIBLE keepsakes, new and old

Janie Craun

Foreword by Wayne Jackson

D1402042

Books with Class

PUBLISHING DESIGNS, INC.
Huntsville, Alabama

Publishing Designs, Inc.
P.O. Box 3241
Huntsville, Alabama

Quotations and lesson texts are from the New American
Standard Bible (1977) unless otherwise noted. I have
occasionally used the Living Bible in order to paraphrase
a speaker's words.

Many of the "Points to Ponder" are anonymous quotations.
Whenever possible, the originator is noted.

Publishers Cataloging-in-Publication Data

Craun, Janie
Heirlooms: Bible keepsakes old and new./Janie J. Craun; foreword by Wayne Jackson.
172 pp.; 22.86 cm.
Includes footnotes, thirteen famous Bible questions, photographs.
1. Women—Religious life. 2. Christian ethics. 3. Christian life.
I. Craun, Janie. II. Title.
ISBN 0-929540-33-6
248.8

Printed in the United States of America

To the memory of my mother,
Rubye Hardeman Porch Jackson

"Poor indeed is the man whose mind is not enriched by some phrase of lasting truth and beauty which serves to restore his soul in the exigencies of life. Each of us needs in his heart's treasury the memory of a lovely line to renew fellowship with the great and noble of this earth—"

Leaves of Gold

". . . in whom [Christ] are hidden all the treasures of wisdom and knowledge."

Colossians 2:3

Contents

God's loving plan of redemption is somewhat like a sparkling stream. Beginning as a bubbling spring in Eden, with the promise of Him who ultimately would crush Satan's head (Genesis 3:15), it rushes on, centuries later pouring its refreshment into the city of Jerusalem with dynamic force. This culmination was on the day of Pentecost—just fifty days following the resurrection of our Savior, Jesus Christ (Acts 2).

The study of how that torrent developed, gaining momentum across the landscape of antiquity, is the most thrilling adventure in the annals of literature.

In her book *Heirlooms*, Janie Craun has traced that "water course" that was carving an eternal niche in providential events of time. And she has done so in a rather unique manner—by probing certain penetrating "questions" that were posed along the way, in the various epochs of biblical history.

From Cain's sarcastic query, "Am I my brother's keeper?" to Pontius Pilate's evasive, "What then shall I do with Jesus?"— questions by biblical personalities are employed as stepping stones in the centuries-long trek.

Questions are intrinsic to human nature. Unlike the beasts of the field, human beings are inquisitive creatures. We raise inquiries, and long to know the answers. Some questions are generated from devout hearts; others (like those cited above) are mere rhetorical devices fashioned to rationalize disingenuous conduct. In any event, questions are marvelous teaching devices.

This book is a wonderfully illuminating sketch of redemptive history. It evinces a great deal of research, is buttressed with practical applications, and is written in an engaging style that does not weary the person of spiritual inclination.

I am delighted to commend this volume most enthusiastically.

~

On a crisp February morning in the eighth year of my life, I was playing with schoolmates on the grounds of my old grammar school in Old Hickory, Tennessee—just a couple of hundred yards from the house in which our family lived. I saw our old Plymouth pull up to the home place, and my mother and dad exit the car. "Momma" was carrying a tiny bundle— my new baby sister, Janie.

That sweet child grew up to become the remarkable Christian woman who authored this book.

Wayne Jackson
Stockton, California

1. **Wayne Jackson**
2. **Janie Jackson Craun**

From Generation to Generation

1. Mom, Rubye Porch Jackson
2. Mom, Dad, Wayne, and Diane
3. Granddaddy and Grandmammy, Clayton and Annie Tipton Jackson
4. Dad, Harry Boyd Jackson, age 5
5. Mama and Papa Craun, Charles Craun
6. Janie

Dear Reader,

Are you an heirloom collector? I am. Almost to the point of clutter! Old photographs, dishes, furniture. Even my great-grandparents' silver communion cup has found a treasured place in my home.

I save partly from a sense of nostalgia but also because these relics from the past help me better understand who I am. Karl and I live on land that belonged to his grandparents. All around us are precious reminders of who we are and from where we have come.

In the same way, the Bible is a treasure-trove for those willing to delve into it. It reveals our privileged ancestry as children of an all-powerful God, and it equips us for the needs of today.

A number of years ago, when a close friend lost her mother suddenly, we undertook the task of cleaning out her attic. That necessity was made more pleasurable as each nook and cranny began to yield the unexpected. We discovered keepsakes she had loved and forgotten, packed alongside items that were practically new. I have often thought of that experience when reading Matthew 13:52, where the Lord said, "Therefore every scribe instructed concerning the kingdom of heaven is like a householder who brings out of his treasure things new and old" (NKJV).

In this study we will explore some beautiful heirlooms of Scripture which connect us to the past. Although we face challenges that are unique to our day, the questions that we ask are not new. Those before us struggled with similar queries, and their experiences have been passed on to us as treasures from the past. May we handle these heirlooms with care and pass them on untarnished to generations to come.

Janie Craun

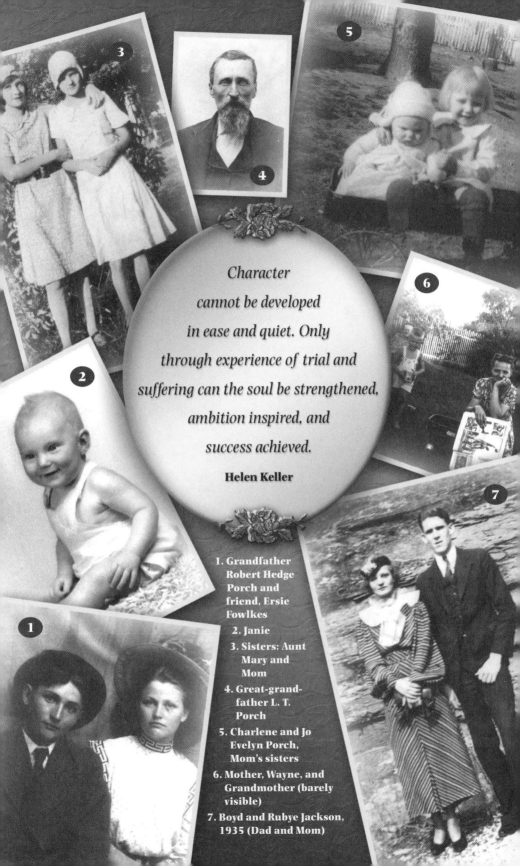

*Character
cannot be developed
in ease and quiet. Only
through experience of trial and
suffering can the soul be strengthened,
ambition inspired, and
success achieved.*

Helen Keller

1. Grandfather
   Robert Hedge
   Porch and
   friend, Ersie
   Fowlkes
2. Janie
3. Sisters: Aunt
   Mary and
   Mom
4. Great-grand-
   father L. T.
   Porch
5. Charlene and Jo
   Evelyn Porch,
   Mom's sisters
6. Mother, Wayne, and
   Grandmother (barely
   visible)
7. Boyd and Rubye Jackson,
   1935 (Dad and Mom)

Am I My Brother's Keeper?

Jimmie Andrews Newman and Linda Meacham Crosslin

Comedian Flip Wilson's famous line was, "The devil made me do it!"
That excuse did not work for Eve; neither will it work for us. Personal freedom
obligates each of us to live with the consequences of our behavior.

"I will not let any man reduce my soul to the level of hatred."

Booker T. Washington

Then the Lord

said to Cain, "Where is

Abel your brother?" And he said,

"I do not know. Am I my

brother's keeper?"

Genesis 4:9

Am I My Brother's Keeper?
A Lesson on Responsibility

Genesis 4:1–26

A Perfect World Lost

Paradise Gained

The Gospel writers credit Moses with the first five books of the Old Testament, known as the Pentateuch. In chapters 1 and 2 his eloquent account of the creation depicts a beautiful and perfect world where all the personalities of the godhead were present (Genesis 1:2, 26; John 1:1–3; Hebrews 1:1–2). God measured time by the passing of evening and morning, and ever since, we have observed the seven-day week, a fact which evolutionists are hard pressed to explain.

Moses wrote about God's creating man—"Adam" or "red earth"—and giving him a garden home in Eden (Genesis 2:8). It was a paradise in which all the wonderfully unique animals He created mingled with Adam, who gave each a name. But when the man realized that there was no one in all of creation like himself, God made a special companion for him from one of his ribs as he slept. She was like Adam, yet delightfully different.

Woman, which is what Adam called her, was not an afterthought on God's part. By creating the man first, God established the principle of male leadership in the home—and later in the church—according to 1 Timothy 2:12–13. Perhaps God also delayed woman's creation so that Adam would experience the loneliness that endeared her to his heart. With pleasure Adam exclaimed, "This is now bone of my bones and flesh of my flesh; she shall be called Woman because she was taken out of Man." In Genesis 2:24 Moses recorded God's timeless intent for marriage, repeated by Jesus in Matthew 19:5: "For this cause a man shall leave his father and mother, and shall cleave to his wife; and the two shall become one flesh." God told the couple to be fruitful, multiply, fill the earth and subdue it, and to have dominion over every living thing.

The Bible account of the first home paints a picture of perfection. Six times Moses states that everything God made was good or very good. Genesis 3 presents a great contrast with the entrance of sin into their perfect world.

Paradise Lost

God chose to make the human couple significantly different from the animals when He created them in His own image and gave them the intelligence to make choices (Genesis 1:27). With that privilege came responsibility, and God would test whether they would act responsibly by giving them one restriction. They were allowed full rein in Eden; only the tree of the knowledge of good and evil that grew in the center of the garden was off limits. One day the serpent visited with the woman and stirred within her a strong desire to taste its beautiful fruit. Genesis 3:1–6 tells how he deceived her into thinking she could disobey God without any consequences.

We understand all too well our adversary's power, because the apostle John writes that we fall victim to his same devices (1 John 2:16). Although Adam was not deceived by the serpent's lies, he made a decision to join his wife in disobedience.

After they had violated God's instructions, the couple experienced a sense of shame they had never known. They realized they were naked and sewed fig leaves together in an attempt to cover themselves. Sin had deprived them of all dignity and security and caused them to be afraid. (Genesis 3:10 is the first mention of fear in the Bible.) It is not hard to imagine the problems that must have developed almost immediately in their home. Likely there were words of discord, for neither of them wanted to take full responsibility for what they had done. We have to wonder: if this perfect woman, married to the perfect man and living in a virtual paradise, was so easily deceived, is there any hope for us in this very imperfect world? We shall see in the lessons to follow that there is indeed hope.

Oh, the Consequences!

They were driven from the beautiful garden, and Adam had to toil by the sweat of his brow to make the soil produce. God had warned him about death (Genesis 2:17), and from that day their bodies began a process of aging which would eventually return them to dust. These were the natural consequences of their disobedience, and they were hard consequences.

Contrary to the tempter's claims, they had seen that God keeps His word. So it must have lifted their wounded spirits when God made a magnificent promise. He foretold that in time the woman's Seed would utterly destroy the devil; and He placed a curse upon the serpent, through whom he had worked. Woman would be saved, so to speak, through the great responsibility and privilege of motherhood, for it was through woman that the divine would take on human flesh and enter the world (Galatians 4:4; 1 Timothy 2:15).

Adam renamed his wife Eve, meaning "life," because she was to become the mother of all humanity. After their union, Eve conceived and bore a son named Cain. She exclaimed, "I have gotten a manchild with the help of the Lord." Later she gave birth to another son, Abel. It is unlikely that Eve realized the sorrow that lay in store for her family. How could she have known that one of her sons would become the murderer of his own brother, because sin had entered into the world?

Out of Control

When Cain and Abel grew to manhood, each assumed an occupation, Abel as a keeper of sheep and Cain as a farmer. In the process of time (literally, "after a considerable lapse of time") they both came before the Lord with offerings. Cain brought a gift of his produce; Abel sacrificed an animal from his flock.

Two things are significant about Abel's gift. Not only did he choose from the firstlings of his flock, but it was the very best he had. Keil and Delitzsch, in their *Commentary on the Old Testament,* give the Hebrew construction as "the fattest of the firstlings, and not merely the first good one that came to hand."[1] "And the Lord had regard for Abel and for his offering: but for Cain and for his offering He had no regard" (Genesis 4:4–5). In this first instance of worship recorded in the Bible, it is noteworthy that God accepted one man's effort while rejecting the other.

We may wonder why God refused Cain's offering. It appears that there were instructions from God which Abel obeyed but Cain did not, based on Hebrews 11:4. "By faith Abel offered to God a better sacrifice than Cain." Romans 10:17 teaches that faith results from adherence to divine instruction: "So faith comes from hearing, and hearing by the word of Christ." We do know that God was looking at Cain's attitude as well as his action. Acceptable worship has always involved doing the right thing in the right spirit (John 4:24).

Which of God's laws did the tempter misrepresent to Eve? (Galatians 6:7–8)

_____

_____

_____

_____

_____

---

1. C. F. Keil and F. Delitzsch, *Commentary on the Old Testament,* vol. 1 (Grand Rapids: Eerdmans, 1978), 90.

Sin on the Prowl

God questioned Cain, "Why are you angry? And why has your countenance fallen?" He warned Cain that he was about to be overtaken by sin. Genesis 4:7 is the first use in Scripture of that word. The depiction of sin as a wild beast lurking at the door for an opportunity to enter Cain's heart is similar to Peter's description of Satan's walking about as a roaring lion seeking its prey (1 Peter 5:8).

I can recall a haunting story from my childhood about two children, living on the frontier and left alone temporarily by their parents. The youngsters were cautioned sternly to keep their cabin door locked. But hours later, the sound of scratching at the door prompted them to open it just a crack. It was enough to allow a ravenous bear to attack them. The story illustrates God's warning to Cain that sin was crouched at his door, looking for an opportunity to overtake him. Satan is always on the prowl, looking for those he can overtake (Galatians 6:1), and it is our responsibility to keep the door shut.

Blood on the Ground

God pointed the finger of blame squarely at Cain. Your offering would have been accepted, God told him, if you had done well. But Cain was not sorry. He spoke to Abel, perhaps luring him to the field; and there he rose up and slew him. The word *slew* signifies being slaughtered or butchered, by cutting the throat.[2] When God asked, "Where is Abel your brother?" his answer was insolent. "I do not know. Am I my brother's keeper?" Having murdered, he was not ashamed to answer God with an arrogant lie.

God told Cain that his brother's innocent blood was crying out from the ground. Justice must be done. Interestingly, the writer of Hebrews noted that the blood of Jesus speaks better things than that of Abel (Hebrews 12:24). His blood whispers peace, according to Edward Bickersteth's well-loved hymn.

Cain became a fugitive in search of a living. He complained that his punishment was greater than he could bear and that he feared being hidden from God, but it seems that he mostly feared revenge. The Lord marked Cain, and lest there be more violence, He promised sevenfold vengeance upon anyone who sought retribution.

We wonder about Cain's state of mind as he left the presence of the Lord and moved eastward. Did he grieve for the younger brother he had slain? Was

---

2. Burton Coffman, *Commentary on 1 John* (Austin: Firm Foundation, 1979), 425.

he ever sorry he had brought such anguish upon his parents? There is no mention of any penitence; and he fathered a race of descendants who introduced polygamy, musical instruments, and implements of brass and iron. Perhaps weapons were among their inventions, since violence clung to his family.

What brought about Cain's downfall?

_____

_____

_____

_____

_____

Eve gave birth to another son, Seth, and there is the suggestion that he was a good boy. Adam, we know, lived long and saw many more sons and daughters grow up before him. Did Eve ever see her wayward son again? There is no record in the Bible. It appears that some of Cain's female descendants intermarried with their distant relatives, which later led to a decline of their good morals (Genesis 6:1–2). Don't you suppose she searched her soul to understand what had happened to her family? Opening the door to sin had changed her world forever.

Who, Me?

What if I can't help how I feel?

I am responsible for controlling my emotions.

Cain's insolent question is troubling. The apostle John wrote that Cain slew his brother "because his works were evil and his brother's righteous" (1 John 3:12 NKJV). Cain was consumed with anger, envy, resentment, and even hatred for Abel (1 John 3:13). How do we respond when these same emotions come knocking on our door?

David declared in Psalm 139 that we humans are "fearfully and wonderfully made." We possess a wide range of feelings and emotions, which the adversary is adept at using to gain entrance into our hearts.

Solomon wrote that there is "a time to love, and a time to hate" (Ecclesiastes 3:8). There is also a time to feel angry, as long as we remain in control. When Moses felt outraged over the actions of the rebellious Israelites, God understood because He was also provoked (Exodus 32:10, 19). It wasn't *feeling* angry that got Moses into trouble. It was how he responded to his anger by disobeying God that created problems for himself (Numbers 20:8–12).

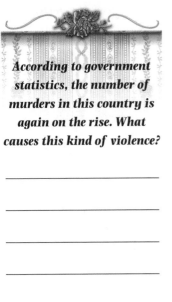

According to government statistics, the number of murders in this country is again on the rise. What causes this kind of violence?

_____

_____

_____

_____

_____

Anger often stems from envy. This green-eyed monster characterizes a corrupt mind, according to Romans 1:29, and is found in company with wickedness, deceit, and hypocrisy (1 Peter 2:1). Envy also leads to resentment, which damages the body as well as the spirit. One physician reported on personal interviews with patients suffering from colitis. The most prominent personality characteristic noted by the interviewers was resentment, occurring in ninety-six percent of the victims.[3]

Unchecked emotions like envy and resentment inevitably result in hatred. The apostle John warned that when we fail to love one another, we are in danger of becoming like Cain, adding that everyone who hates his brother is a murderer (1 John 3:15). Jesus explained that the prohibition against murder in Moses' law would be unnecessary if everyone would control his anger against his brother (Matthew 5:21–24). We would do well to adopt the philosophy of Booker T. Washington, a man who knew the brunt of prejudicial malice but vowed, "I will not let any man reduce my soul to the level of hatred."

I am accountable for my actions.

The lesson of Cain is that we are accountable for our actions. Under the law of Moses, every transgression and disobedience received a just penalty (Hebrews 2:2). The gospel of grace brought hope into the world; but this prompted some in Paul's day to think they could keep living in sin, and God would overlook it. Not so, according to Romans 6:1–2. God holds each person responsible for the choices he makes (Acts 17:30; Hebrews 2:2–3).

Furthermore, God has required accountability in every age, even from those not in a covenant relationship with Him (Romans 1:18–19; 2:14–15). Every civilization has morés of right and wrong, which illustrates that we humans expect responsible behavior from others, even if we are sometimes

---

3. S. I. McMillen, *None of These Diseases* (Old Tappen, NJ: Revell Co., 1980), 68.

willing to overlook our own failures (Matthew 7:1–5). Comedian Flip Wilson's famous line was, "The devil made me do it!" That excuse will not work for us any more than it worked for Eve.

I must deal responsibly with my mistakes.

> *What is wrong with "passing the buck"? Everyone does it!*

The responsible way to deal with transgressions is to confess them (1 John 1:9). David lusted for another man's wife, which led him to commit adultery and murder. Until he came to terms with his sin, he suffered mental and physical anguish, as recorded in Psalm 51. His actions were reprehensible, but he acknowledged them and repented with bitter tears. In Psalm 32 he poured out his deep gratitude for God's forgiveness. There was no way for him to undo all the consequences of his behavior; but God forgave him, and his penitence resulted in these beautiful psalms which have brought comfort to so many others.

I must live with the consequences of irresponsible behavior.

In Hebrews 11, the great faith chapter, the writer records that Moses chose to suffer affliction rather than enjoy the "pleasures of sin for a season" (Hebrews 11:25 KJV). No doubt about it; sin is pleasurable! Satan has found a way to appeal to every appetite (1 John 2:16), but there is a price to be paid.

Our society is reaping the fruits of an "anything goes" mentality. Behaviors once considered irresponsible have become acceptable. Although they have always been with us, today they are "out of the closet." As a result our nation is plagued with diseases, addictions, unwanted pregnancies, and disrespect for human life. Like our Grandfather Adam and Grandmother Eve, we must live with the consequences of our sins and the resulting guilt of unconfessed sin.

> *Why must I confess my failures and shortcomings? (1 John 1:8–10)*

In his classic book *Whatever Became of Sin?* Dr. Karl Menninger suggests that although the word *sin*

How does my view of human origin affect my understanding of personal responsibility?

_____

_____

_____

_____

_____

_____

has almost disappeared from our vocabulary, a sense of guilt remains that has afflicted the world with the depression, gloom, discouragement, and apprehensiveness that is so prevalent.[4] Irresponsibility has created a stressed-out generation in which violence is a far-too-common response.

One prominent politician, in commenting on the violence in some of our schools, has suggested that it is the result of our "evolutionary heritage." The Scriptures do not support this explanation. Violence erupts when human emotions are not governed by the limits set by God. Personal freedom obligates each of us to live with the consequences of her behavior. Without personal responsibility, the consequences will always make society a very dangerous place.

---

4. Karl Menninger, *Whatever Became of Sin?* (New York: Hawthorne Books, 1973), Book Jacket.

Points To Remember

◆ I am responsible for controlling my emotions.

◆ I am accountable for my actions.

◆ I must deal responsibly with my mistakes.

◆ I must live with the consequences of irresponsible behavior.

Points To Ponder

◆ *Freedom is a package deal—with it comes responsibilities and consequences.*

◆ *When you take responsibility on your shoulders there is not much room left for chips.*

◆ *"We become what we are as persons by the decisions that we make." Aristotle*

◆ *"Responsible persons are mature people who have taken charge of themselves and their conduct, who own their actions and own up to them—who answer for them." William Bennett,* The Book of Virtues

2

Is Anything Too Hard for the Lord?

Great-grandmother, Eliza Wade Hardeman

Even though Sarah laughed at God's promise,
her actions indicated that she believed He would keep it.

*"By faith even Sarah herself also received ability to conceive . . .
since she judged Him faithful who had promised."*

Hebrews 11:11

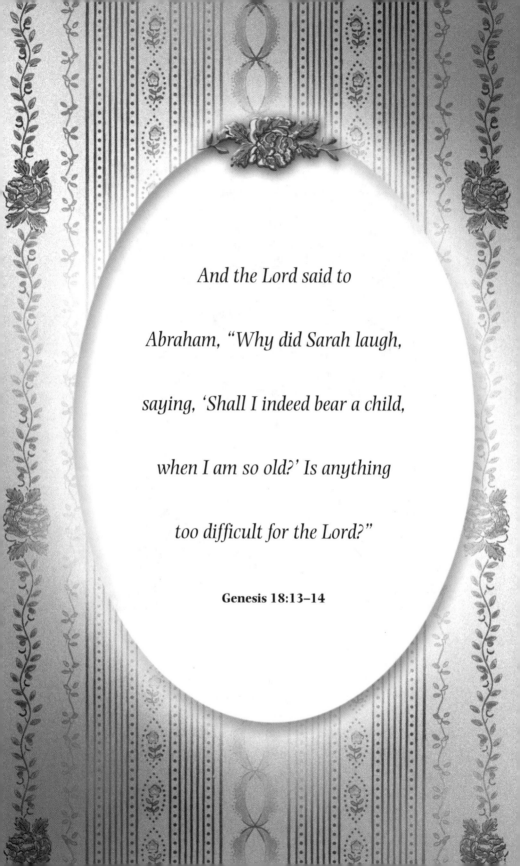

And the Lord said to

Abraham, "Why did Sarah laugh,

saying, 'Shall I indeed bear a child,

when I am so old?' Is anything

too difficult for the Lord?"

Genesis 18:13–14

Is Anything Too Hard for the Lord?

A Lesson on Faith

Genesis 17:1–18:14

God's Promise Renewed

A Growing Family Tree

The story of Abraham and Sarah might well begin in the Garden of Eden with the promise God made to Adam and Eve. Before He banished them from the garden, God foretold the coming of the woman's Seed who would destroy the adversary, later called Satan. According to the record, some nineteen generations elapsed before God spoke again about that promise.

After Adam and Eve left Eden, the earth's population began to multiply rapidly. Adam lived 930 years with seven generations of descendants who were remarkable in their longevity. One of them, Methuselah, lived to the ripe old age of 969. It must have concerned Adam to see his offspring becoming increasingly corrupt due to the wickedness that surrounded them.

In time God grew weary of striving with people whose every thought was evil (Genesis 6:5), and He announced His intention to destroy what He had created. Peter tells us that He "preserved Noah, a preacher of righteousness, with seven others, when He brought a flood upon the world of the ungodly" (2 Peter 2:5). Shem, a son of Noah who survived the flood, was the ancestor of Abram.

We first read of Abram in Genesis 11, which lists him as the ninth generation from Shem. The long lifespans of Abram's ancestors indicate that all nine generations were still living at the time of his birth! It is possible that Abram received his account of the flood from these elderly patriarchs. And it may help to explain how he maintained his faith in God while living among idolatrous people.[1]

A Man of Faith

Abram was one of three brothers who lived in Mesopotamia about 2000 B.C. Their father Terah, like the majority of people in their home of Ur of the Chaldees, worshiped other gods (Joshua 24:2). Abram was married to his half-sister Sarai, also the daughter of Terah by another wife (Genesis 20:12). Two brothers, Haran and Nahor, completed the family unit, with Nahor being

---

1. William Smith, *Old Testament History* (Joplin, MO: College Press, 1978), 24-27.

married to his niece Milcah (Genesis 11:29). So it was a very close-knit family. Marriage within the family was later forbidden under the law of Moses (Leviticus 18).

The city of Ur was at one time the greatest city of the known world. Archaeology reveals that it was a center of trade and manufacturing, located west of the Persian Gulf near the intersection of the Tigris and Euphrates rivers where its situation made it ideal for farming. Excavations have uncovered evidence of two-story brick dwellings, libraries, schools, and shops with imported goods.[2] But the people of Ur were idolatrous, and worship to the moon-god and his counterpart dominated the city. In the Temple-Tower, which was a structure resembling a pyramid, Ur's citizens practiced religious prostitution.[3] According to Acts 7:3, God called Abram away from that environment saying, "Depart from your country and your relatives, and come into the land that I will show you." The writer of Hebrews declares that Abram obeyed by faith, "not knowing where he was going" (Hebrews 11:8).

A Gentle Spirit

Sarai is one of the most prominent women in the Bible. She was beautiful, ten years younger than Abram (Genesis 12:14; 17:17). Together they shared a faith in God that was truly remarkable. Peter states that Sarai possessed a gentle and quiet spirit that prompted her to submit to her husband's leadership (1 Peter 3:1–6). So when Abram announced that they were leaving Ur to venture to an unknown land, she was willing to go.

After a sojourn in Haran, where Terah died, Abram and Sarai gathered up their possessions and servants, and with their nephew Lot, set out for the land of Canaan. Abram was seventy-five years old, and God had promised to make him great and the father of a great nation through whom all families of the earth would be blessed. For the next twenty-five years, the two wandered throughout the land, living in tents and trusting God to fulfill His promise.

At first Sarai must have anticipated that she would be the mother of Abram's children. But as the years unfolded and she failed to conceive, she suspected that God had a different plan. Abram was thinking about making his house steward his heir when God intervened and assured him that the promised seed would issue from his own body. Still, God made no mention of Sarai's role.

---

2. Henry Halley, *Halley's Bible Handbook* (Grand Rapids: Zondervan, 1965), 87-89.
3. Ibid., 95.

It was probably with great disappointment that she therefore proposed to Abram that they employ a practice which was common in their day. She would allow her Egyptian handmaid Hagar to bear a child *for* her. The child that was conceived would legally be Sarai's.[4] Without seeking God's direction, Abram consented and, at the age of eighty-six, fathered a son, Ishmael.

A Promise Believed

When Ishmael was thirteen, God again appeared to Abram and renewed the promises He had made four other times. It was on this occasion that God changed his name to Abraham, for He said, "I will make you the father of a multitude of nations" (Genesis 17:5). And then God made what must have been a most astounding announcement:

> As for Sarai your wife, you shall not call her name Sarai, but Sarah shall be her name. And I will bless her, and indeed I will give you a son by her. Then I will bless her, and she shall be a mother of nations; kings of peoples shall come from her (Genesis 17:15–16).

Abraham was dumbfounded. He fell on his face before God; but inwardly he was laughing in astonishment and thinking, "Will a child be born to a man who is one hundred years old? And will Sarah, who is ninety years old, bear a child?" Cautiously, Abraham wondered if Ishmael might not become his heir.

God's reply was unmistakable. "No, but Sarah your wife shall bear you a son, and you shall call his name Isaac [laughter]; and I will establish My covenant with him for an everlasting covenant for his descendants after him" (Genesis 17:19). God went on to assure Abraham that his son Ishmael would become a father of princes. But he was not the son of promise. To think that Sarai could conceive a child at this point in her life required much faith. Here God left Abraham to ponder the astonishing news.

As a symbol of His covenant, God required Abraham to undergo the rite of circumcision. At the age of ninety-nine, Abraham had himself circumcised along with every male in his household, including the servants. His obedience demonstrates that he believed God could and would keep His promise.

A Mother of Nations

Shortly thereafter, Abraham received a visit from three strangers. Hospitality was of great importance among Easterners, so Abraham immedi-

---

4. Wayne Jackson, *Bible Studies in the Light of Archaeology* (Montgomery, AL: Apologetics Press, 1982), 2.

ately ran to meet them and bowed himself to the ground. He was evidently still a strong and vigorous man! He offered water and refreshment while Sarah prepared freshly baked bread, veal, and milk. After dinner they inquired about Sarah's whereabouts, because she had remained out of sight in the tent but listening to their conversation. One of the visitors said to Abraham, "Sarah your wife shall have a son."

Inside the tent door, Sarah laughed! After years of trying to conceive, the probability of motherhood now seemed incredulous. "After I have become old, shall I have pleasure, my lord being old also?" she wondered (Genesis 18:12).

The visitor, identified as the Lord, said to Abraham, "Why did Sarah laugh, saying, 'Shall I indeed bear a child, when I am so old?' Is anything too difficult for the Lord?" Sarah hurried forward to protest, "I did not laugh," but like her husband, she certainly had, and the Lord corrected her saying, "No, but you did laugh!"

Before leaving Abraham's home, the messengers revealed disturbing news to the patriarch. They warned him of the impending destruction God was going to bring upon the wicked cities of the plain where their nephew Lot was living. In the weeks that followed, Abraham moved his household farther south and sojourned in Gerar for several months. Sarah must have retained some of her remarkable beauty, for the king of Gerar even wanted her for his harem until he discovered that she was Abraham's wife.

How was Isaac's name appropriate?

Soon thereafter, God empowered Sarah with the strength to conceive a child. The writer of Hebrews states, "By faith even Sarah herself also received ability to conceive, even beyond the proper time of life, since she considered Him faithful who had promised" (Hebrews 11:11).

A Promise Embraced

The child of promise was born at last, and Isaac became the light of his mother's life for thirty-seven years. As a young man he possessed the same submissive spirit found in his parents. The Jewish historian Josephus believed Isaac to be twenty-five years old when he accompanied Abraham to Mount Moriah and consented to being bound and placed upon an altar.[5] It seems at least likely

---

5. William Whitson, *Complete Works of Flavius Josephus* (Grand Rapids: Kregel Publications, 1977), 36-37.

that he was old enough to have resisted had he not possessed a faith like that of his father who trusted in the power of God to raise him up (Hebrews 11:19).

Sarah did not live to see the fulfillment of God's promise to make of Isaac a great nation because he did not marry until after his mother's death. But the writer of Hebrews reveals that she saw these promises afar off and embraced them (Hebrews 11:13). (What a beautiful verse!) She contented herself to live the nomadic life with Abraham while she waited for a city with foundations "whose builder and maker is God" (Hebrews 11:10 KJV).

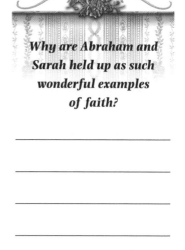

Why are Abraham and Sarah held up as such wonderful examples of faith?

To focus upon the mistakes of Sarah and Abraham is to miss the lesson of their remarkable faith. Even though they laughed at God's wonderful promise, their actions indicated that they believed He would keep that promise. W. H. Bathurst penned the words of this famous hymn,

> Lord, give us such a faith as this;
> And then whate'er may come,
> We'll taste e'en here
> The hallowed bliss of an eternal home.

Who, Me?

I do believe, but . . .

Faith accepts the unseen.

The writer of Hebrews defines faith as "the assurance of things hoped for, the conviction of things not seen" (Hebrews 11:1). He explains that faith helps us understand that the visible things of this world came into being by means of things that are invisible, being formed by the word of God (Hebrews 11:3). Paul observed that one of the great paradoxes of life is that "the things which are seen are temporal, but the things which are not seen are eternal" (2 Corinthians 4:18). The trials we face in this life should help us focus on the eternal rewards which are visible only through faith. The ability to believe in the unseen promises of God has always characterized the faithful. In order to please God, we must have confidence in His ability to provide the rewards He has promised (Hebrews 11:6).

Why is it so hard to believe in the unseen?

_____

_____

_____

_____

_____

Faith obeys.

Hebrews 11 is often referred to as "Faith's Hall of Fame." It is like strolling through a museum of great Bible characters whose lives exemplified their trust in God. In this chapter we read about such personalities as Noah, Abraham, Sarah, Isaac, Jacob, Joseph, Moses, and many others too numerous to mention. The writer mentions more than a dozen people who were motivated by faith or through faith. By faith Noah prepared an ark; by faith Abraham obeyed; by faith Moses chose to suffer affliction and forsook Egypt. It seems clear that the writer intended to emphasize the relationship between faith and obedience to God's will.

Paul wrote that Abraham is the father of all who believe and who "follow in the steps" of that faith (Romans 4:12). He explains that it is not the outward symbol of circumcision that characterizes a true believer, but it is faith "working through love" (Galatians 5:6). The righteous live by faith (Hebrews 10:38). Apparently some in the early church misunderstood the nature of faith, for James shows that the faith of our father Abraham became perfect through his obedience. He concludes that justification before God results from submission to His will and not from mere intellectual faith. James 2:21–26 is the only reference in the Bible to "faith only" (v. 24 KJV), and it clearly teaches that "faith without works [of obedience] is dead."

How do we know that faith involves obedience?

_____

_____

_____

_____

_____

The famed Baptist evangelist Charles Spurgeon once wrote, "Faith and obedience are bound up in the same bundle. He that obeys God, trusts God; and he that trusts God obeys God. He that is without faith is without works; and he that is without works is without faith."[6]

Faith Accepts God's timetable.

David wrote in Psalm 33:20, "Our soul waits for the Lord; He is our help and our shield." Speaking through the prophet Zephaniah, God foretold a time of restoration for spiritual Israel in these words, "Therefore wait for Me, declares the Lord" (Zephaniah 3:8). God has His own timetable for fulfilling His promises. He is not bound by time as we know it (Psalm 90:4; 2 Peter 3:9).

If God loves me, why does He make me wait?

Adam and Eve had no way of knowing that several thousand years would elapse before the arrival of the promised Seed. God sent Him when the fullness of the time had come (Galatians 4:4). God does not forget about His promises, and faith must learn to wait on Him.

Faith sustains.

In times of great stress, faith provides the strength to endure. David wrote, "I would have lost heart, unless I had believed that I would see the goodness of the Lord in the land of the living" (Psalm 27:13 NKJV). The apostle Paul wrote to Timothy from his prison cell in Rome, where he awaited execution, and stated with confidence: "I have fought the good fight, I have finished the race, I have kept the faith" (2 Timothy 4:7 NKJV). Because of that, Paul was ready for the trial that lay ahead of him. Someone once said that "faith gives us the courage to face the present with confidence, and the future with expectancy." Faith sweetens life with the assurance that we can leave our prayers in the hands of a Father for whom nothing, indeed, is too hard.

Recall a time when faith upheld you.

---

6. Clyde Francis, ed., *Leaves of Gold* (Williamsport, PA: Coslett Publishing Co., 1948), 66.

Points To Remember

- Faith accepts the unseen.
- Faith obeys.
- Faith accepts God's timetable.
- Faith sustains.

Points To Ponder

- *Genuine faith is assuring, insuring, and enduring.*
- *All men need a faith that will not shrink when washed in the waters of affliction and adversity.*
- *God makes a promise—faith believes it, hope anticipates it, and patience quietly awaits it.*
- *Every tomorrow has two handles. We can take hold of it by the handle of anxiety, or by the handle of faith.*

3

Who Am I That I Should Go?

Bible Class – N. B. Hardeman, teacher
Georgie Robertson Christian College
now Freed-Hardeman University
c. 1910 – 1911

God has a role in mind for each of us that often requires
us to leave our comfort zone. Sometimes we,
like Moses, become pretty good at making excuses.

"When duty calls, some people
are never home."

Anonymous

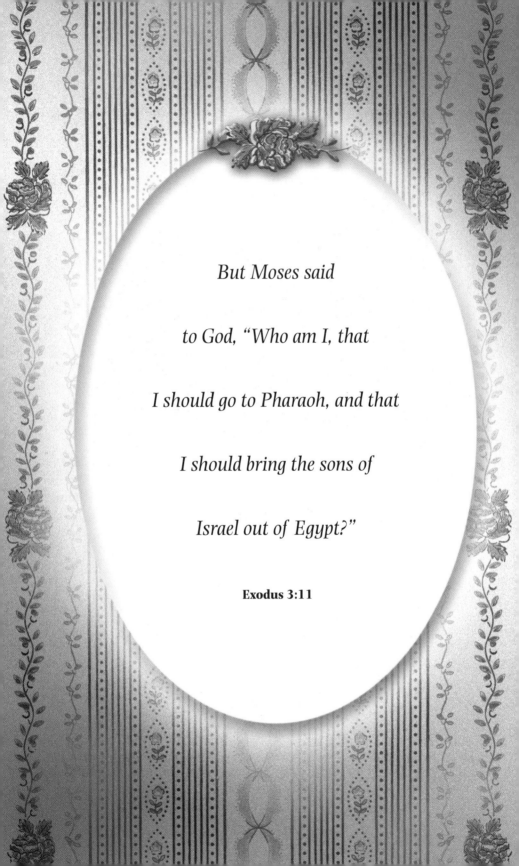

But Moses said

to God, "Who am I, that

I should go to Pharaoh, and that

I should bring the sons of

Israel out of Egypt?"

Exodus 3:11

Who Am I That I Should Go?

A Lesson on Service

Exodus 3:1–4:17

The Promise Unfolds

A Suitable Daughter-in-Law

God's promise to Abraham began to unfold at the birth of Isaac. After the death of Sarah, Abraham sought a wife for Isaac among their kinsmen in Padan-Aram. She must be a companion who shared his faith in God, because together they would begin building a nation through whom all families of the earth would be blessed. His prayers for a suitable daughter-in-law were answered when God led Abraham's steward to the home of his brother Nahor.

You will recall that Nahor's wife Milcah was both niece and sister-in-law to Sarah. Nahor and Milcah were grandparents of a beautiful girl named Rebekah (Genesis 22:20–23), who agreed to the marriage proposal (Genesis 24:57–58). Although Isaac was then a mature man of forty, he loved Rebekah the moment he saw her. At their marriage, he gave her the tent that had been Sarah's for her own in that new country, far removed from her family.

As she studied her new home, she must have wondered about the mother-in-law she had never known. She might have imagined Sarah's apprehension at leaving a familiar land to sojourn in tents. In time she came to feel Sarah's disappointment when she realized that she, too, was barren. Isaac entreated the Lord on her behalf, and God heard his prayer. After twenty years of marriage, Rebekah conceived twin boys (Genesis 25:20–26).

A Plan of Deception

The sons, Jacob and Esau, were competitive from birth, and their parents only aggravated the problem by playing favorites. When the boys grew to young adulthood, their competition created a family crisis. Esau, born first, was entitled to the birthright and the special blessing of the firstborn; but God had revealed to Rebekah before their birth that the elder would serve the younger.

Perhaps Rebekah saw qualities in her son Esau that led her to a plan of deception. She directed Jacob to trick his father Isaac, whose eyesight had grown dim, into bestowing the privileges of the first-born upon himself. Understandably, Esau was upset. The writer of Hebrews says he was an immoral and godless person and suggests that he became embittered (Hebrews 12:15–16).

Although he later reconciled with his brother, his descendants would forever bear a grudge. (See the book of Obadiah.)

Rebekah hurried Jacob away to her brother's home for a short visit to let Esau's anger cool (Genesis 27:42–44). Little did she realize that twenty years would elapse before his return. It is unlikely that she ever saw Jacob again; she never knew her grandchildren who were born in Padan-Aram. Like Sarah, she had run ahead of God, and in the process she created a problem in her home. (Read Genesis 28:6–9.) The poet was right:

> O, what a tangled web we weave,
> When first we practice to deceive!

Sowing and Reaping

When Jacob was fleeing from his brother Esau, he camped in a place which he afterward named Bethel 'house of God', and there in a vision the Lord made him the same promise He had made to Abraham and Isaac. The vision had a profound impact upon Jacob and prompted him to vow that he would serve the Lord if God would bless and protect him. God did bless Jacob richly, so that he eventually returned home with a large family and many possessions. On the way, God appeared to him again and changed his name from Jacob to Israel which means "having power with God."

Repeatedly, the Scriptures bear out the truth that "whatever a man sows, this he will also reap" (Galatians 6:7). The deception Jacob had practiced as a youth returned to haunt him years later when his own favorite son, Joseph, was sold into Egyptian slavery by his older brothers. They deceived their father into thinking that Joseph had been killed by a wild animal.

Genesis 39–45 recounts how Joseph's faith and the Lord's providential care over him flourished in Egypt. He rose to a position of power second only to the Pharaoh himself. Ancient Egyptian hieroglyphs mention a Minister of the Interior and Superintendent of Granaries which probably closely resembled Joseph's position.[1] He eventually reunited with his penitent brothers and brought the entire clan, near seventy in number, to live in the land of Goshen (Genesis 46:27). The area was isolated from the Egyptians who despised shepherds, but it was rich pasture land and afforded them the privacy to practice their own customs and religion. There Abraham's seed grew into a nation that

---

1. William C. Martin, *These Were God's People* (Nashville: Southwestern Co., 1996), 9-50.

numbered in excess of 600,000 men, according to Numbers 1:46. God's plan was unfolding.

Archaeology has uncovered Egyptian texts which record seven-year famines, the distribution of food from royal granaries, and an influx of foreigners known as the Habiru, generally believed to be Hebrews.[2] According to Exodus 1:8, a new king arose in Egypt who did not favor Joseph. Because he saw Israel as a threat, the new ruler began a systematic persecution of the Hebrew people. They were forced into slavery; and when that did not diminish their numbers, all male babies were slaughtered. It was during this period of "ethnic cleansing" that Moses was born.

Moses: The First Forty Years

Through a scheme that involved great faith on the part of his mother, Moses survived and became the adopted son of Pharaoh's daughter. Hebrews 11:23 commends the faith of both his parents, saying that when they saw their beautiful child, they were not afraid of the king's edict. The princess reared him as an Egyptian, with his own Hebrew mother serving as nurse.

Life must have been difficult for Moses, living in two worlds and belonging in neither. Perhaps there were whispers and sneers behind his back from those in Pharaoh's court. In Goshen, his favored position must have been an affront to many in the slave community. But Moses was drawn to identify with his own people; and when he caught an Egyptian beating one of them, he slew the Egyptian and became a wanted man. His own kinsmen turned on him, and Moses had to flee the country altogether. Hebrews 11:27 records that "he left Egypt, not fearing the wrath of the king; for he endured, as seeing Him who is unseen."

Moses: The Second Forty Years

At the age of forty, Moses found refuge in the land of Midian, a desert area inhabited by Bedouin nomads. Far removed from his former life of royalty, he married and started a family and lived another forty years as a simple shepherd. Very likely he spent long days in physical labor, meditating on his eventful life and the plight of his people. Moses didn't know it, but God was preparing him for the greatest challenge of his life.

---

2. Martin, *God's People*, 54.

With the rise of a new ruling class in Egypt, life became more oppressive for the Israelites.

> And the sons of Israel sighed because of the bondage, and they cried out; and their cry for help because of their bondage rose up to God. So God heard their groaning; and God remembered His covenant with Abraham, Isaac, and Jacob (Exodus 2:23–24).

One day Moses was keeping the flocks of his father-in-law Jethro in a barren wilderness near the mountain called Horeb. His attention focused upon the sight of a strangely burning bush. As he drew closer, a voice identifying Himself as the God of Abraham, Isaac, and Jacob spoke to Moses. He commissioned him to return to Egypt and lead his people out of bondage and back to the very mountain where he stood.

Called to Serve

Moses was not at all eager to take on that challenge and protested with a series of excuses. "Who am I, that I should go to Pharaoh, and that I should bring the children of Israel out of Egypt?" he inquired. He considered himself inadequate for the task, but God replied, "I will certainly be with you."

Moses argued, "What shall I say to them?" When God rehearsed for Moses the exact message he was to take to the Pharaoh, he continued: "Suppose they will not believe me or listen to my voice?" Although God showed him miraculous signs that would compel them to believe, Moses was still fearful and protested, "O my Lord, I am not eloquent." The Lord replied, "Who has made man's mouth? Or who makes him dumb or deaf, or seeing or blind? Is it not I, the Lord?" (Exodus 4:11). He promised Moses, "I, even I, will be with your mouth and teach you what you are to say." Moses had no more excuses to offer and so in essence he said, "Lord, please! Send someone else" (LB). God's patience was tried, but He allowed Aaron, the brother of Moses, to serve with him as his spokesman.

Later, Moses was called the meekest man on the face of the earth (Numbers 12:3). W. E. Vine comments that this quality of meekness is a characteristic of the spirit in which "we accept [God's] dealing with us as good, and therefore without disputing or resisting."[3] The Greek word *prautes* signifies total submission of one's strength and will into the hands of a superior. Although Moses did not quality for the accolade at the burning bush, the experiences in Egypt, and

---

3. W. E. Vine, *An Expository Dictionary of New Testament Words*, vol. 3 (Old Tappen, NJ: Revell 1966), 55.

later in the wilderness, would lead him to a deeper dependence upon Jehovah. By allowing God to use him, Moses the shepherd would eventually become Moses the deliverer and lawgiver, one of the greatest men in all of recorded history (cf. Hebrews 3:1–6).

Can't someone else do it?

The thankful want to serve.

The years in Midian probably had passed uneventfully, and Moses' mind must have dwelt at times on his early life in Egypt. Perhaps he wondered why God had spared his life when other innocent babies were being slaughtered. No doubt he thought often about the advantages he had known as a prince in a rich and powerful nation. Twice delivered from death, he had enjoyed many blessings. These thoughts may have turned his heart closer to God. Romans 2:4 asserts that God's goodness has the power to bring about a change of life.

Acts 9 records the conversion of Saul of Tarsus, later called Paul, who met the Lord on his journey to Damascus where he was going to seek out and arrest Christians. The encounter with the risen Christ left him trembling and asking, "Lord, what do You want me to do?" (Acts 9:6 NKJV). He followed God's instructions to be baptized and became a chosen vessel to bear the name of Jesus to many (Acts 9:6–19). Aware of the debt he owed, Paul wrote, "Christ Jesus came into the world to save sinners, of whom I am chief" (1 Timothy 1:15 NKJV). Like Moses, Paul was chosen by God for a great and costly mission, and he would not refuse. He, too, went on to achieve a greatness he could never have envisioned.

Consider the worldly woman whose sins were forgiven by Jesus. She was so overwhelmed by His kindness that she washed His feet with her tears and anointed them with costly perfume. Jesus explained to His critics, "Her sins, which are many, have been forgiven, for she loved much; but he who is forgiven little, loves little" (Luke 7:47). Once we have tasted God's goodness and grace, we become energized. We want to serve, even if it demands sacrifice.

One of the most beautiful passages in the Bible, Philippians 2:5–8, talks about the servant nature of Jesus. He did not cling to His equality with God, although He could have, but emptied Himself and took on the form of a bondservant while in the flesh. He often referred to Himself as the Son of Man, a term that emphasized His humanity. The Son of God told His disciples that He had not come to be served, but to serve, and to give His life a ransom for many (Matthew 20:28). It was hard for the apostles to understand, because the principle that the greater must serve the lesser is contrary to human nature. They were more concerned about which of them was the greatest (Luke 22:24).

Service demands sacrifice.

God warned Moses that delivering the Israelites would be no easy task because Pharaoh would not want to let the people go. Moses also found that it would involve personal sacrifice. It seems that his wife Zipporah did not understand the call her husband followed. Perhaps she felt threatened by his return to Egypt; and she resented the circumcision of her son, which Moses evidently had neglected until then (Exodus 4:24–26). As a result, Zipporah and her two boys returned to her father and did not accompany Moses to Egypt.

Why is it important for new Christians to find work in the church?

_____

_____

_____

_____

_____

Many a good person has been hindered in serving God by family members who are not supportive. Abraham was certainly wise in seeking a wife for his son among those of like faith. His grandson Esau did not follow his good example and married several women, some of them ungodly. The nation of Edom which he fathered was a thorn in the flesh to God's people for generations until God destroyed them.

It is clear that God wants us to meet our family responsibilities (Matthew 10:37–38). But Jesus taught, in the clearest possible language, that serving Him is our first priority (Luke 14:26). Those who plan to become active Christians after they have reared their families and retired from their life's work are like the man Matthew tells about who wanted to follow Jesus after he had met his family obligations. Jesus urged him to rearrange his priorities (Matthew 8:21–22).

Service results in growth.

One anonymous writer has quipped: "When duty calls, some people are never at home." God has a role in mind for each of us that often requires us to leave our comfort zone. Sometimes we, like Moses, become pretty good at making excuses for ourselves.

We read in Mark about a young fellow who ran to Jesus and knelt before Him inquiring, "Good Teacher, what shall I do to inherit eternal life?" This exemplary young man had kept the commandments as faithfully as anyone could, and Jesus was drawn to him. But the Master saw that materialism was controlling his life, and He challenged him to sell all and follow Him. Sadly, the young man went away grieved, because he had great possessions (Mark 10:17–22). Each of us might ask, "What does Jesus see when he looks into my heart? Is something hindering me from being a better servant?"

Why should the young develop avenues of service early in life?

Moses lacked confidence in his ability, and sometimes this plagues us as well. Jesus addressed timidity in a parable in Matthew 25:14–30. Three servants received varying amounts of money to manage, according to each man's ability. Two of the servants invested wisely and increased their master's profits, but one servant hid his cash in the ground. He was afraid he might make a mistake, and so he opted for what he thought was a safe course—he did nothing! As it turned out, the master would have been more tolerant of poor judgment than slothfulness. He cast that servant out of his service because he was of no use whatsoever.

Jesus called Peter, Andrew, James, and John away from their fishing business, which provided a livelihood for their families and those of their servants, in order to make them fishers of men. Don't you suppose they had some apprehension, even fear, as each of them gave up a familiar lifestyle to undertake a new calling? Not one of them had the benefit of a formal education, yet they became powerful ministers of the gospel after their association with Jesus (Acts 4:13).

Low self-esteem is a crippler which we must work to overcome. For some, that is very hard to do because low self-esteem results from years of negative programming. To say "I'm not good at anything" is worse than false modesty, however. It is to become like the unprofitable servant. Remember, he was not praised for being humble; he was condemned for neglecting his opportunity. Remember also that the ones who used what they had, received more. With opportunity, as with anything else, it's a fact that we "use it or lose it."

What talents have you developed by leaving your comfort zone?

_____

_____

_____

_____

Service brings satisfaction.

Someone has said, "The roots of happiness grow deepest in the soil of service." Jesus found great satisfaction in doing good. On one occasion while traveling from Judea to Galilee, He passed through the town of Sychar, a Samaritan village. He was very weary from walking and stopped by Jacob's well late in the day to rest. While the disciples were in the city purchasing food, He requested a drink from a local woman who came to draw water, and found an opportunity to share with her the good news of the kingdom.

The disciples returned to find, to their surprise, that Jesus had an interest that superceded physical food. "I have food to eat that you do not know about," He said. "My food is to do the will of Him who sent Me, and to accomplish His work" (John 4:34). By ministering to her needs, He had satisfied other needs of His own.

Do you agree that giving results in more happiness than receiving? Why?

_____

_____

_____

_____

A well-known psychologist was asked what he would recommend for a person suffering from temporary depression. He replied that he would suggest helping someone less fortunate. It is difficult to feel unhappy when we are busy bringing joy to others. Many young people today suffer from depression, and an alarming number are committing suicide. Some teens have everything that money can buy, yet they are empty inside. Sadly, no one has taught them the joy of serving others. It is wonderful to see Christian youth voluntarily giving their time to help the needy of the congregation or the community. They are learning early the truth of Jesus' statement, "It is more blessed to give than to receive" (Acts 20:35).

When Moses asked, "Who am I that I should go?" God promised, "I will be with you." He obeyed God and became a great leader. More important, to God he became "my servant, Moses."

Points To Remember

◆ The thankful want to serve.

◆ Service demands sacrifice.

◆ Service results in growth.

◆ Service brings satisfaction.

Points To Ponder

◆ *Service is love in work clothes.*

◆ *It is not always the talented people who serve the Lord best—it is the consecrated ones.*

◆ *It is better to have a little ability and use it well than to have much ability and make poor use of it.*

◆ *"The noblest question in the world is, 'What good may I do in it?'" Benjamin Franklin*

4

Who Is on the Lord's Side?

Mother and Janie

When the church tolerates immorality, the result is a lowering
of spiritual standards, which left uncorrected will spread like leaven.
And when an entire nation condones and even approves an immoral
lifestyle, it will eventually result in anarchy; those who disregard
God's laws of morality will not long honor any laws.

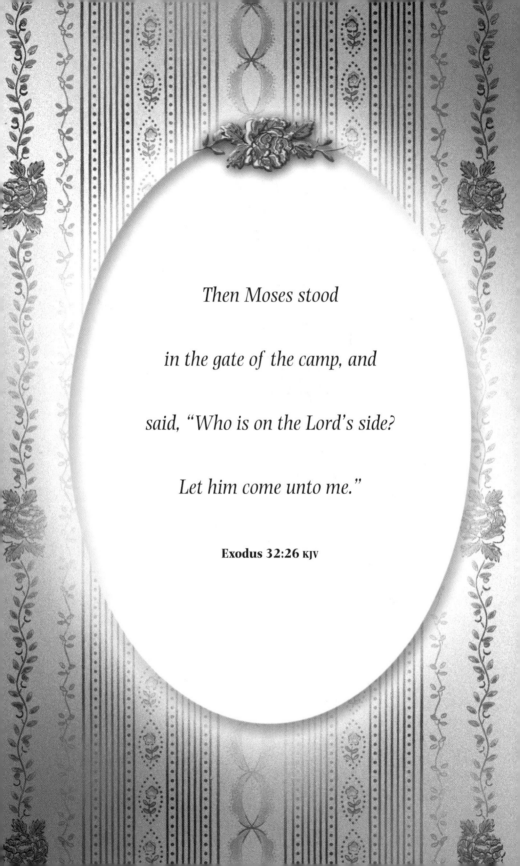

Then Moses stood

in the gate of the camp, and

said, "Who is on the Lord's side?

Let him come unto me."

Exodus 32:26 KJV

Who Is on the Lord's Side?

A Lesson on Morality

Exodus 32:1–35

Moses: The Last Forty Years

The Great "I AM" Revealed

As Moses journeyed back to Egypt, many thoughts must have occupied his mind, not the least of which was how his people were going to receive the message he was bringing. God's promise to Abraham was 430 years old, and it is unclear just how well the people knew the God of their fathers. Not only must Moses convince the Pharaoh to believe him; he also must rekindle the faith of Abraham, Isaac, and Jacob within the hearts of his own kinsmen.

He would first tell the Israelites that the God of their fathers had revealed Himself in the burning bush as "I AM WHO I AM." (Most English Bibles translate God's name as YHWH or JHWH, since these are the consonant letters in the verb "I AM." Because the original Hebrew language contained no vowels, the name is generally pronounced "YAHWEH" or "JEHOVAH.") As soon as they arrived in Egypt, Moses and Aaron met with the Hebrew elders to tell them about Jehovah's plan to deliver them from captivity.

The promise of freedom and the miraculous signs produced faith in the Israelite leaders, but it was a conditional faith. They were not yet prepared to have it tested. They had been immersed in false religion for so many generations they had much to learn about the Lord. Those who expected immediate release were soon disappointed because Pharaoh, who did not recognize the Hebrew deity, was unmoved by Moses' plea and was not about to lose a slave force that numbered half a million men. He asked Moses, "Who is the Lord, that I should obey His voice to let Israel go? I do not know the Lord, and besides, I will not let Israel go" (Exodus 5:2).

In return, Pharaoh oppressed the Israelites more than ever by demanding that they find their own straw for the bricks used in his construction projects. When the people were unable to keep up their quotas, Pharaoh had the Hebrew overseers beaten. The people's budding faith turned into resentment against Moses and Aaron, whom they blamed for making their lives even more miserable (Exodus 5:20–21).

Moses himself was discouraged and asked the Lord, "Why is it You have sent me? For since I came to Pharaoh to speak in Your name; he has done evil

to this people; neither have You delivered Your people at all" (Exodus 5:22–23 NKJV). God assured Moses that His plan would be accomplished and would cause Israelite and Egyptian alike to recognize that He was Lord (Exodus 6:7; 7:5).

A Great Contest

There began a contest of wills between Pharaoh and Jehovah. Time and again Moses and Aaron entered Pharaoh's court with the demand that he release the people; but each time the king's heart grew harder, and he refused to let them go. Jehovah brought ten terrible plagues upon Egypt before Pharaoh's stubborn will yielded. Each plague, more destructive than the last, demonstrated to the Egyptians that their deities were no match for the God of Israel.

He turned their water to blood. He smote them with frogs, lice, and flies. He sent a deadly epidemic among their cattle followed by painful boils which broke out upon the people. The land was destroyed by hail and locusts, killing vines and figs and trees (Psalm 105:33). All of this devastation preceded three days of pitch darkness, in which the Egyptians were unable to move about.

As a final demonstration of His power, God would perform a deed so terrible as to strike fear in the hearts of the Egyptians and demonstrate His providential care for the descendants of Abraham (Exodus 11:7; Psalm 105:38). On the fourteenth day of the month Nisan—our March–April—each Hebrew household was to sacrifice a yearling lamb or kid and apply its blood to the lintels and doorposts of their houses. When He saw the blood, Jehovah would pass over the homes of the saved. Inside their houses, Hebrew families ate the roasted meat with unleavened bread as part of the Passover, the beginning of a memorial that would be observed throughout their generations (Exodus 12:14).

At midnight, anguished cries rang throughout Egypt as every firstborn died, from the eldest in Pharaoh's palace to the firstborn of the animals in the stalls. Only in Goshen did calm prevail as God's people made hurried preparations to depart. Before dawn Pharaoh sent an urgent message telling the Israelites to go and sacrifice to God, adding, "And bless me also" (Exodus 12:32). The Israelites were laden with gifts of gold, silver, clothing, and other valuables as they quickly left the land of their captivity.

The Exodus

Had they followed the most direct route, they would have arrived in Canaan, the home of their ancestor Abraham, in a matter of days. God, however, knew that this mass of people, some two million to three million in number, was weak and undisciplined. So Moses directed them back to the mount of God where Jehovah made ready to reveal Himself to them. God continued to demonstrate His power through marvelous signs and wonders, leading them during the day in a pillar of cloud and by night in a pillar of fire (Exodus 13:20–22).

Meanwhile, Pharaoh, whose heart had hardened once more, pursued Israel with six hundred chosen chariots as far as the Red Sea. Moses commanded the people, "Do not fear! Stand by, and see the salvation of the Lord" (Exodus 14:13). According to God's instruction, Moses lifted his rod and the waters parted. Israel crossed on dry ground. Then at Moses' word, the sea retreated and Pharaoh's entire army perished in a watery grave, so that "the people feared the Lord, and they believed in the Lord and in His servant Moses" (Exodus 14:31).

For three days they marched forward through the Wilderness of Shur until thirst overcame them and the Lord provided water. When their bread ran out, God rained manna from heaven. Although He supplied their every need, God allowed them to know hunger and thirst so that they might understand that "man does not live by bread alone, but man lives by everything that proceeds out of the mouth of the Lord" (Deuteronomy 8:3). With each crisis, however, their faith wavered; and although they murmured and complained until God's patience wore thin, Jehovah was true to His promise. He brought them out of Egypt "with a mighty hand and an outstretched arm and with great terror and with signs and wonders" (Deuteronomy 26:8). After three months, the throng of Israelites arrived at Mount Sinai.

The people had long been waiting for the day when they would assemble in that awesome place to serve God (Exodus 3:12), and so with great expectation they watched Moses ascend the mountain to receive God's instructions. When he returned they were told to purify their bodies and to set boundaries around the mountain, lest any man or animal intrude upon the holy ground and perish.

On the third morning they awoke to thick clouds full of thunder and lightning. The whole mountain quaked, and the servant Moses ascended Mount Sinai amid fire and smoke to meet with Jehovah. At his return, God spoke His laws in the hearing of the people in a voice so deafening that everyone trembled greatly and pleaded with Moses to speak for God lest they die.

Nothing had prepared the Israelites for what they witnessed at Sinai. Moses said to the people, "Do not be afraid; for God has come in order to test you, and in order that the fear of Him may remain with you, so that you may not sin" (Exodus 20:20). The test which Israel was about to experience would demonstrate just how weak their faith was.

Unrestrained

When Moses returned to God on Mount Sinai, he remained there forty days, receiving all of God's instructions for the new nation. As days passed into weeks, the people grew restless and fearful; at length they revived the old idolatrous practices they had known in Egypt. They petitioned Aaron to make them an image, saying, "As for this Moses, the man who brought us up from the land of Egypt, we do not know what has become of him" (Exodus 32:1). How quickly they turned on Moses and forgot the One who had really delivered them from bondage.

Surprisingly, Aaron took their golden earrings and fashioned them into the molten image of a calf, similar to the Egyptian Apis, or bull-god. They proclaimed it a representation of the god who had brought them up from Egypt. It is impossible to fathom what was in Aaron's mind as he built an altar and announced that on the morrow they would feast "to the Lord."

Camped in the middle of a rugged wilderness, the massive horde of exiles was impatient to reach the land of promise. Weeks of waiting for Moses to return left them disgruntled. Perhaps Aaron sensed their restlessness and was afraid for his own life. Whatever his intent, his proposal of a feast put the crowds into a festive mood; and early the next morning they commenced to bring sacrifices and burnt offerings to the place of worship. They began to celebrate with food and drink and music. They became intoxicated and began singing and dancing and reveling, which according to McGarvey, "was the common accompaniment of idolatry."[1] Soon their behavior was totally out of control (Exodus 32:6; 1 Corinthians 10:7–8).

As their carousing continued, Moses returned from Mount Sinai with the *Ten Commandments* on tables of stone, written by the finger of God (Exodus 31:18). Realizing what the people were doing, he threw down the tablets, sym-

---

1. J. W. McGarvey and Philip Pendleton, *Thessalonians, Corinthians, Galatians, and Romans* (Delight, AR: Gospel Light), 100.

bolically destroying the very laws that the people were breaking. Turning to Aaron, Moses demanded an explanation; Aaron offered the lame excuse that all he had done was to cast their offerings into the fire, and "out came this calf."

Then Moses stood in the gate of the camp and shouted, "Who is on the Lord's side? Let him come unto me" (Exodus 32:26 KJV). Only those in Moses' own tribe of Levi joined him, and they assumed the difficult task of meting out punishment to certain of the offenders by executing three thousand men. Because Moses interceded for the people, God spared the rest; nevertheless He smote the entire camp with a plague (Exodus 32:35).

Who, Me?

I'm just doing what everyone else does!

Those who assembled at the base of Mount Sinai were like people in every age. Some in the mixed multitude which followed Israel out of Egypt likely had no faith in Jehovah at all (Exodus 12:38). Others in the crowd possessed a very weak and immature faith, enthusiastic only as long as they were not being tested. Some who appeared strong proved to be a disappointment. Only a small minority possessed enough faith to do as God commanded.

What are some things that cause a heart to be hard toward God?

In Matthew 13 Jesus pictured these same types of individuals in the parable of the sower. It is still true today that some who hear will never accept the truth; their hearts are too hard. Others make an eager start but quickly fall away; their roots are too shallow. There are those who seem to be steadfast until the cares of the world pull them away. In the words of Jesus, relatively few develop a mature, saving faith—a sobering thought! (Matthew 7:13–14).

We have already learned that obedience is a matter of personal responsibility. Some have charged that since the Scripture states that God hardened Pharaoh's heart (Exodus 7:3 KJV), He must have predestined him to be impenitent. But we know that God

wants all people to come to repentance (2 Peter 3:9). Someone has observed that the same sun hardens clay and melts butter. No one can blame God for a hard heart.

Immorality stems from unbelief.

Exodus 32:25 records that Moses found the people "out of control" when he returned from the mount. They had thrown off all restraint and were engaging in indecent acts. In our own day the expression "do your own thing" characterizes the attitude of many people toward reckless behavior. Our society is so accustomed to a lack of self-control, many see it as normal.

When Peter wrote about those who pursue a course of "sensuality, lusts, drunkenness, carousals, drinking parties and abominable idolatries" (1 Peter 4:3), he was describing the life some early Christians had left behind when they came out of paganism. These shameful activities are routine for many in our own society on any given weekend. We are becoming a licentious people. Webster defines licentiousness as "lack of moral restraint, lasciviousness." It falls in the category of sins which Paul terms "works of the flesh" (Galatians 5:19–21) and which will keep one out of the kingdom of heaven. In his discourse in Romans 1, Paul notes a progression within societies from ignorance, ingratitude, and idolatry to immorality. Those who refuse to be restrained, he writes, are on a collision course with destruction.

Leaders can make a difference.

Thank God for strong leaders! Someone has observed, "The business of a leader is to turn weakness into strength, obstacles into stepping stones, and disaster into triumph." These are tall orders. Moses became such a leader, although he shied away from the calling. On the other hand, Numbers 12:1–2 seems to indicate that both Aaron and his sister Miriam wanted leadership roles, but God rejected their self-will.

Throughout the period of the judges, and later the kings, the Israelites pretty much rose or fell according to the quality of their character. Godly leaders were a great blessing—men like Gideon, Samuel, David, Joash, and Josiah come to mind. Others were infamous for their idolatrous practices and the immorality that flourished. Jeroboam, Ahab, and Manasseh were among them.

Civil and spiritual leaders often prove to be weak and disappointing. During the reign of Ahab and Jezebel, the prophet Elijah felt like giving up until God reminded him that He still had seven thousand faithful. Later, New Testament Christianity thrived despite efforts of Nero, one of history's most depraved emperors, to destroy it. It isn't easy, but people of faith can survive a corrupt government.

Our pilgrim forefathers saw themselves as candles, kindled for the purpose of lighting a nation.[2] Today our society as a whole ridicules puritan ideals, and it is unpopular to speak out against behaviors that the Bible labels sin. People no longer commit adultery; they engage in affairs. Fornication has been renamed "recreational sex." Within some schools, textbooks present homosexuality as an alternative lifestyle, and the school nurse may dispense a contraceptive, but not an aspirin. And there is a staggering epidemic of alcohol abuse on college campuses, because social drinking has become a normal rite of passage to adulthood.

What creates an immoral society?

Even under weak leaders, the influence of each Christian can make a difference. The famous motto of the Christopher Society—"It is better to light one candle than to curse the darkness"—was first taught by Jesus in Matthew 5:16.

It is disappointing that Aaron did not speak up and challenge the immoral activities all around him. He might have made a difference. But what about our own timidity? A 1996 poll reported that "public distress about the state of our social morality has reached nearly universal proportions: eighty-seven percent of the public fear that something is fundamentally wrong with America's moral condition."[3] Think what a change would occur today were eighty-seven percent of us willing to take a stand! Someone is watching my actions, as well as yours. We need to follow the example of the early Christians who prayed for boldness to speak the truth (Acts 4:29).

It's been said that a good leader takes a little more than his share of the blame and a little less than his share of the credit. We don't expect perfection in our leaders, but we do admire those who take responsibility seriously. The Lord's

---

2. William Bradford, *Of Plymouth Plantation*, (n.p., n.d.), 21.
3. William J. Bennett, *The Death of Outrage* (New York: The Free Press, 1998), 35.

people have an obligation to pray for those in authority, even when we disagree with their decisions (1 Timothy 2:1–3).

Ritual is no substitute for righteousness.

Moses wrote that "the people sat down to eat and to drink, and rose up to play" (Exodus 32:6). Their immoral behavior followed a period of worship. It was not authorized by God, but in the eyes of the people it was worship, nevertheless.

Think of the atrocities that have occurred throughout history in the name of religion. Leaders have authorized holy wars, religious prostitution, even human sacrifices. Many people have assumed that religious ritual has the power to absolve sin. The prophet Isaiah had harsh words for those who went through the motions of worship while they had every intention of continuing immoral practices. God said to them, "So when you spread out your hands in prayer, I will hide My eyes from you, yes, even though you multiply prayers, I will not listen" (Isaiah 1:15). He required that they remove the evil from their lives before He would pardon them (v. 16).

Immorality defiles those who embrace it.

Finally, we must remember that Israel's behavior brought consequences upon the nation as a whole. Three thousand died by the swords of the Levites. As for the golden calf, Moses burned it with fire, ground it into powder, and scattered it into the brook of water from which they drank. Had Moses not interceded for the people, falling prostrate before God, Jehovah would have destroyed them all, including Aaron (Deuteronomy 9:18–20). The message from God clearly demonstrated that He would not tolerate immoral behavior in individuals or in the nation as a whole.

Proverbs 14:34 says that "righteousness exalts a nation: but sin is a disgrace to any people." Immorality has entered our homes through the media

Why is it often difficult to find individuals willing to lead, in any capacity?

What was the religious climate of Isaiah's day, and does it resemble the views of many today?

and through parental neglect to teach children standards of right and wrong. There it has resulted in rebellion. Wherever the church tolerates immorality, it results in a lowering of spiritual standards which, left uncorrected, will spread like leaven (1 Corinthians 5:6). And when an entire nation condones and even approves an immoral lifestyle, it will eventually result in anarchy; because those who disregard God's laws of morality will not long honor any laws.

What effects of immorality are evident in our world?

_____

_____

_____

_____

_____

- ◆ Immorality stems from unbelief.
- ◆ Leaders can make a difference.
- ◆ Ritual is no substitute for righteousness.
- ◆ Immorality defiles those who embrace it.

- ◆ *Virtue has more admirers than followers.*

- ◆ *Without strong moral motivations, freedom develops into license and license into anarchy.*

- ◆ *Vice is a monster of such frightful mien,*
  As, to be hated, needs but to be seen;
  Yet seen too oft, familiar with her face,
  We first endure, then pity, then embrace.
  —Alexander Pope, Essay on Man

- ◆ *"It is far worse to excuse wrongdoing, watch ethical standards sink, and allow justifiable outrage to die than to confront wrongdoing." William Bennett*

- ◆ *Forbidden fruits result in many jams.*

- ◆ *"Flee immorality. Every other sin that a man commits is outside the body; but the immoral man sins against his own body. Or do you not know that your body is a temple of the Holy Spirit who is in you, whom you have from God? And that you are not your own: for that you have been bought with a price; therefore glorify God in your body" (1 Corinthians 6:18–20).*

5

Obeying the Voice of the Lord?

Great-grandparents John and Ludie Tipton
Grandmammy Annie, first on left, and siblings

Religious division might be resolved if everyone aimed
to worship God only as He has authorized.

"God is greatly to be feared in the assembly of the saints,
and to be held in reverence by all those who are around Him."

Psalm 89:7

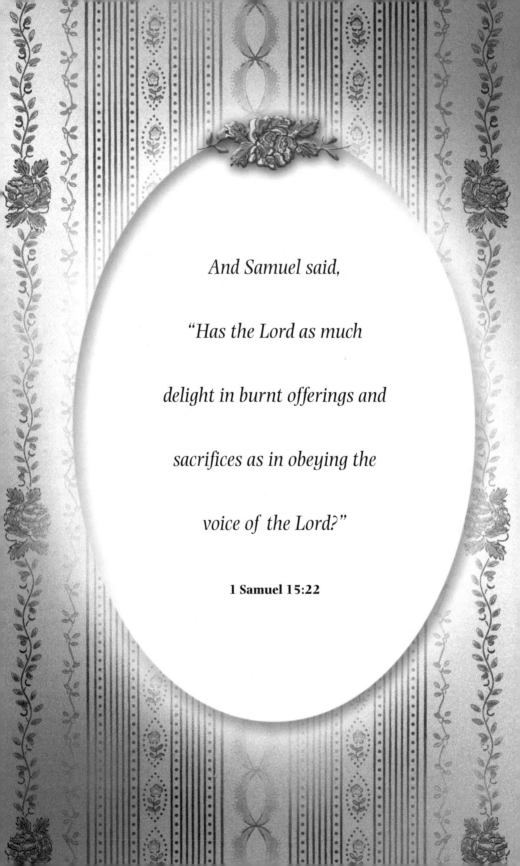

And Samuel said,

"Has the Lord as much

delight in burnt offerings and

sacrifices as in obeying the

voice of the Lord?"

1 Samuel 15:22

Obeying the Voice of the Lord?
A Lesson on Worship

1 Samuel 15:1–35

The Wilderness Wandering

Love the Lord

After Moses had destroyed the golden calf, he ascended the mountain bearing two more tables of stone. For a second time he communed with God and received His written covenant with Israel.

> Then God said, "Behold, I am going to make a covenant. Before all your people I will perform miracles which have not been produced in all the earth, nor among any of the nations; and all the people among whom you live will see the working of the Lord, for it is a fearful thing that I am going to perform with you. Be sure to observe what I am commanding you this day" (Exodus 34:10–11).

God delivered to Moses the *Ten Commandments*, otherwise known as the Decalogue or the "ten words." The first four taught the Israelites about God's unique nature. The children of Israel were to be unlike the other nations, who worshiped many deities; they were to have no other gods besides Jehovah. As they learned from making the golden calf, they must not represent Him by any man-made image nor in any way abuse His holy name. At this time God designated the seventh day as a day of rest—the Sabbath.

They were also commanded to honor their fathers and mothers. In the New Testament, disobedience to parents characterizes an unholy people who no longer acknowledge God nor any other authority (Romans 1:28–30; 2 Timothy 3:2).

Love Thy Neighbor

These commandments preceded five rules for governing their relationships with others. It is interesting that the "experts" insist that small children require rules which are stated in the positive, rather than the negative, and that parents are obligated to satisfy every "why." Israel was an infant nation, and God's commandments were simple prohibitions: "Thou shalt not" commit murder, adultery, theft, false witness, and covetousness. To those living in the Christian Age, the *Sermon on the Mount* teaches an expansion of those principles.

Parents who tell their children "no" firmly but kindly, and reinforce the message when necessary, are not warping their young minds. Little ones can understand the meaning of "no" long before they comprehend why certain behaviors are inappropriate.

Civilized people recognize that these basic rules from God are essentials for living together in society. The *Ten Commandments* spelled out what Cain had not understood: that it matters how we attempt to reverence God, and that one is required to be his brother's keeper. Jesus said these truths form the basis for all the other commandments (Matthew 22:36–40).

Observe the Heavenly Patterns

There were also laws directing the construction of a tabernacle of worship to reside in the center of the camp. God gave very specific instructions regarding it, because the tabernacle and the worship were a type—a copy or shadow—of heavenly things. So God told Moses, "See . . . that you make all things according to the pattern which was shown you on the mountain" (Hebrews 8:5; Exodus 25:9, 40). We will see that there were very severe consequences for those who presumed to alter God's pattern.

Israel remained at Sinai for a full year before Jehovah signaled that it was time to resume their journey to Canaan. When the cloud moved forward, Israel traveled through the barren and desolate wilderness of Paran, described by Moses as "a great and terrible wilderness" (Deuteronomy 1:19). Although they were impatient to reach the land of Canaan, many hardships lay ahead. They did not realize that the tests of their faith would parallel the experiences of all who embark upon a journey with Jehovah (1 Corinthians 10:1–11). The wilderness became a type of the Christian life, from their baptism in the waters of the Red Sea until the final crossing over the river Jordan and entrance into the promised land. Their struggles are a source of instruction and hope as we make our own sojourn through life (Romans 15:4).

Proceed in Faith

While Israel was camped at Kadesh-barnea not far from the borders of Canaan, twelve men were sent into its fertile valleys to spy out the land and its inhabitants. One man from each tribe participated in a forty-day fact-finding expedition. They returned with mixed reports. All agreed that the land was wonderful, "flowing with milk and honey," and to prove their point they brought back ripe figs and an enormous cluster of grapes (Numbers 13:23–27). Ten of the spies, however, came to the conclusion that they could not prevail against its large, fortified cities. And the inhabitants appeared as giants, they said, beside whom they were no more than grasshoppers, hence the term "grasshopper complex." Only Caleb, of the tribe of Judah, and Joshua, of the tribe of Ephraim, were optimistic and told the people, "We should by all means go up and take possession of it, for we shall surely overcome it" (v. 30).

God saw that the faith of this people was still far too weak to trust Him; and not only that, they rebelled against Moses and Aaron and planned to stone them to death and choose a new captain to lead them back to Egypt. As a result, God turned them back into the wilderness, determined that all who had rejected Him should die in the desert. He would wait to fulfill His promise when the next generation came of age.

At this stage the Israelites were like little children in need of discipline (Hosea 11:1, 7). They had flaunted their independence and refused to listen to Jehovah. And then, when they had to be punished, they cried and begged for Him to relent. Deuteronomy 1:45 says that God did not listen to them. In other words, He let them take their punishment. What a great lesson for parents today! Had God given in to their tears and allowed their disobedience to go unpunished, they would never have grown into a nation capable of making the tough decisions they would later confront.

For thirty-eight more years, the Israelites sojourned in the desert while a new generation emerged who was more inclined to obey God. That generation did enter the land, though not under the leadership of Moses. Even he experienced a lapse in obedience and was allowed only to gaze into the land of promise from Mount Nebo, where he died and was laid to rest by the hand of God (Deuteronomy 34:5). God had already chosen Joshua, a man of faith and courage, to succeed him (Numbers 27:18–22).

Before his death, Moses delivered a great discourse to the people in which he urged them to remember the lessons of the past. He delivered the book of the law to the Levites with instructions to "place it beside the ark of the covenant of the Lord your God, that it may remain there as a witness against you" (Deuteronomy 31:26). His famous address should be repeated to people of every generation as a reminder of the importance that God places upon obedience (Hebrews 5:8–9).

Enter the Promised Land

Under the leadership of Joshua, the people entered the land of promise and began to claim it. One by one, its many kings with their fortified cities fell before Israel's armies until, after several years, they had subdued the land. Joshua would later record:

> So the Lord gave Israel all the land which He had sworn to give to their fathers, and they possessed it and lived in it. And the Lord gave them rest on every side, according to all that He had sworn to their fathers, and no one of all their enemies stood before them; the Lord gave all their enemies into their hand. Not one of the good promises which the Lord had made to the house of Israel failed; all came to pass (Joshua 21:43–45).

The land was divided among the twelve tribes, and the Israelites enjoyed peace and prosperity as long as they obeyed God. But the young nation was like the teen who rebels against all that he has been taught once he is out from under the influence of godly parents. The Israelites were faithful to Jehovah only until the death of Joshua and the elders who outlived him (Joshua 24:31). From that point on, they began to "run with the crowd" like the nations around them.

Did Jehovah intend for his instructions to be taken as suggestions or commands?

_____

_____

_____

_____

Spiritual Decline

A new generation arose who did not know Jehovah, and they forsook the God of their fathers to worship Baal and his consort Ashtoreth. God was angry and delivered them into the hands of invaders until they repented and cried for His help. (Read Judges 2:10–23.)

We are reminded of the son in Luke 15 who rebelled against his father and went into a far country. He enjoyed the pleasures of sin for a season before he "came to himself." Not once, but repeatedly, Israel would come to herself, return to Jehovah, and seek His forgiveness and the Lord would raise up deliverers. We marvel at God's great patience in providing help in the form of judges over a period of about three hundred years. There were fifteen judges during this time of spiritual decline, described as a time when "everyone did what was right in his own eyes" (Judges 21:25).

The last judge was a remarkable man who was also priest and prophet. Samuel was born in answer to a mother's prayer for a son whom she might devote to the service of Jehovah. She brought him as a child to the tabernacle, then at Shiloh, where he literally grew up in the house of God. He was a good man whose leadership was a blessing to Israel, but he brought up sons who did not follow in his steps. (What do you suppose their godly grandmother Hannah thought of them?)

When Samuel grew old, the nation demanded that he give them a king. They used the wickedness of his sons as a pretext, but God knew their real desire was to be like the other nations. He told Samuel, "They have not rejected you, but they have rejected Me from being king over them" (1 Samuel 8:7).

The Scriptures teach that God does not prevent us from having our own way. Therefore he sent Samuel to anoint them a king, a young man who was handsome and well built and who towered head and shoulders above the people (1 Samuel 9:2). Their reaction was wildly enthusiastic (1 Samuel 10:24); he certainly looked the part of a king! However, God had Samuel warn them that they would come to regret their demand, and God would not rescue them as He had done in the past (1 Samuel 8:18–20).

King Saul: From Promising to Presumptuous

In the beginning Saul displayed some marks of a promising leader. Samuel himself observed that there was no one quite like him. We immediately note what appeared to be modesty. Samuel had already anointed Saul at God's direction before he assembled the people at Mizpah. When lots were cast and fell upon Saul—which came as no surprise—he had occupied himself amongst the travelers' baggage. He had to be summoned before the people like one who accepts his role with great humility. Then, in one of his first official duties, he demonstrated an attitude of restraint by sparing the lives of several who had opposed him as king (1 Samuel 11:12–13).

Someone once observed: "Many a promising young man has been ruined or reduced to mediocrity, by getting his hands on too much power before he was able to handle it." Saul is a prime example that power corrupts. He was but thirty years old when he began to reign, and with the acquisition of power he became increasingly presumptuous.

Feeling confident, Saul assembled an army to wage war with the Philistines; and the enemy responded with a force "like the sand which is on the seashore in abundance." (1 Samuel 13:15). Saul was eager to attack, but he had been commanded to wait for Samuel to offer sacrifices and bring instructions from God. When Samuel was delayed in coming and some of the troops began to desert, Saul decided to offer the sacrifices without waiting for the go-ahead from God (1 Samuel 10:8; 13:8–9).

The old prophet arrived just as Saul finished and charged him with failing to keep the commandment of God. He prophesied that God would not establish his kingdom but would give it unto another "after His own heart" (1 Samuel 13:14). Saul brooded over this, but it did not stop him from becoming more and more presumptuous. His arrogance led to complete alienation from Jehovah and His prophet during the battle of Amalek.

Samuel had told Saul, "The Lord sent me to anoint you as king over His people, over Israel; now therefore, listen to the words of the Lord" (1 Samuel 15:1). God had given the king great victories, and he was growing confident in his own power. But then God told Saul to execute judgment on the people of Amalek for their treacherous acts against Israel. He expressly commanded that all be destroyed—every person and every animal. Saul disobeyed God's specific command and spared Agag the king and all the best of the cattle and valuables.

Rejected for Disobedience

When Samuel arrived, Saul announced rather defensively that he had obeyed God. From the sounds of the sheep and oxen, Samuel noted that he obviously had not, but the king replied:

> I did obey the voice of the Lord, and went on the mission on which the Lord sent me, and have brought back Agag the king of Amalek, and have utterly destroyed the Amalekites. But the people took some of the spoil, sheep and oxen, the choicest of the things devoted to destruction, to sacrifice to the Lord your God at Gilgal (1 Samuel 15:20–21).

Notice Saul's reasoning. He hadn't disobeyed even though he had not done all that God had commanded him to do. Samuel replied,

> Has the Lord as much delight in burnt offerings and sacrifices as in obeying the voice of the Lord? Behold, to obey is better than sacrifice, and to heed than the fat of rams. For rebellion is as the sin of divination, and insubordination is as iniquity and idolatry. Because you have rejected the word of the Lord, He has also rejected you from being king (1 Samuel 15:22–23).

Saul was quite defensive until he realized that God meant to remove him as king, and at that point he confessed his sin. He implored Samuel to pardon him so that he might worship, and the old prophet accompanied him reluctantly.

But he told Saul, "You have rejected the word of the Lord, and the Lord has rejected you from being king over Israel" (1 Samuel 15:26). Saul was guilty of two grievous sins in God's sight. In the first instance, he went beyond what God had authorized him to do, and in the second, he failed to do all that God said to do. Saul's actions led Samuel to grieve for the unwise king who had showed so much promise, but on that day he broke all ties with Saul.

Isn't worship about how I feel?

Power can result in presumption.

Someone has written that nearly all men can stand adversity; but if you want to test a man's character, give him authority. Perhaps David recognized that truth, for he prayed that God would help him avoid presumptuous sins (Psalm 19:13). Though he was a powerful king, he knew that he must remember to whom he bowed. Presumption is assuming the right to substitute one's own ideas for what God has commanded. It is insubordination—idolatry. God revealed His contempt for it in Deuteronomy 18:20–22 where He required that a prophet who spoke anything on His behalf which He had not authorized should be put to death. Moses, on the other hand, was careful to follow God's instructions for the tabernacle to the letter, even inspecting all the work himself to see that it was done according to God's pattern (Exodus 39:42–43).

What was wrong with Saul's reasoning?

_____

_____

_____

_____

_____

Saul should have remembered Nadab and Abihu, the sons of Aaron who served as priests. Their job was to take censers of burning coals from the altar and sprinkle them with incense as an offering to Jehovah. Their role was one of responsibility and prominence. On one occasion, for some unknown reason, they made a decision to use fire from another source. As a result they were consumed with fire from heaven (Leviticus 10:1–2). What might have seemed to be a minor substitution was sinful in

God's sight. He said: "By those who come near Me I will be treated as holy. And before all the people I will be honored" (Leviticus 10:3).

Later kings of Israel let the power of leadership go to their heads as well. Most notable was Jeroboam, the infamous king "who made Israel to sin," because he made changes in the worship God had authorized. According to

When does change become presumptuous?

_____

_____

_____

_____

_____

1 Kings 12:25–33 he set up golden calves at Dan and Bethel, where he substituted his own priests and changed the feast days to a month "which he had devised in his own heart." His rebellion led God to bring an end to his dynasty (13:34). So also today when people presume to change what God has commanded, they are treading on dangerous ground (2 Peter 3:16).

God has always communicated His will to mankind—at first through the heads of families called patriarchs, then through the law of Moses and the prophets, and finally in Christ (Hebrews 1:1–2). The inspired writings of the New Testament were intended to equip the Christian thoroughly for every need (2 Timothy 3:16–17). Over the centuries, religious leaders in positions of power have presumed to alter the divine plan which was "once for all delivered to the saints" (Jude 3). Note these changes among many:

A.D. 110   Plurality of elders replaced by a single bishop
A.D. 185   Infant baptism added
A.D. 251   Pouring substituted for immersion
A.D. 606   The first universal pope declared
A.D. 667   Instrumental music added to worship
A.D. 1311   Sprinkling authorized[1]

The religious leaders of Jesus' day challenged Him with this question: "By what authority are You doing these things?" (Mark 11:28). Those who presume to go beyond the Scripture must be prepared to answer the same question.

---

1. Phil Sanders, "Evangelism Handbook of New Testament Christianity" (Unpublished, 1997), 5-8.

Partial obedience is disobedience.

Saul thought he could get by with partial obedience, but one does not receive God's blessing until he has completely obeyed. Remember Naaman, commander to the king of Syria, who developed the dreaded disease of leprosy. He responded gladly when he heard that the prophet of God could heal him. His pride did not prevent him from journeying to a nation he felt to be inferior nor from offering to pay a fabulous gift. He was prepared to do almost anything until the prophet instructed him to dip seven times in the river Jordan. The simplicity of such a seemingly ridiculous command offended him (2 Kings 5:11). How many earnest people today will obey God in almost everything the New Testament commands, only to draw the line over the one act of obedience which can wash away their sins! (Acts 22:16).

Worship is God-centered, not man-centered.

The word for worship comes from the Old English *worthship*. It is the means by which we communicate to God our praise, adoration, and dependence upon Him.[2] The Greek word *proskuneo* means to "throw oneself on the ground in respect and awe."

The object of our worship is Jehovah, Who delights in obedience rather than ritual. The citizens of Athens had a shrine for every god imaginable, as though their religious diversity should be applauded. Paul reminded them that the true God does not need the worship of men's hands since He is the giver of all things (Acts 17:25). Our God sits enthroned, lofty and exalted, and will not be enamored with worship designed to please ourselves (Isaiah 6:1–3).

What is the essence of true worship?

_____

_____

_____

_____

_____

Much of the religious division within and without the church might be resolved if everyone aimed to worship God only as He has authorized. We cannot go back and reinstate elements of Moses' law, for it has been replaced by a new law (Galatians 4:9–11; Colossians 2:14; Hebrews 8:6–8, 13). In the areas of preaching, teaching, praying, giving, communing, and singing, the New Testament is the only reliable

2. Jason Jackson, *Christian Courier,* vol. 35, no. 2 (June 1999).

pattern we can follow. If God expected Moses to do all things according to His pattern, why would He expect less of us today?

A well-known fast-food jingle says, "Have it your way." It is tempting to carry this attitude into worship. If we could have it our way and offer God whatever feels right, Cain's worship would have been acceptable. But we must conclude from the commands and examples in the Bible that human additions and substitutions fall under the category of presumptuous sin.

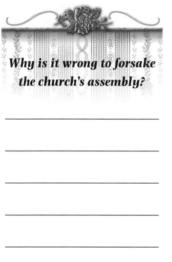

Why is it wrong to forsake the church's assembly?

Worship is a command.

The Scriptures command that we "worship the Lord in the beauty of holiness" (Psalm 29:2 KJV), and we do that both individually and collectively. Worship is a personal activity in which each Christian must sing and make melody in his own heart (Ephesians 5:19), pray with understanding (1 Corinthians 14:15), and individually search the Scriptures to learn what is true (Acts 17:11). He must examine his heart in the taking of the Lord's supper (1 Corinthians 11:28), and give of his means as he has been prospered (1 Corinthians 16:2). Worship is also a joint activity. The Scripture commands that we not forsake the assembling of the church because we all need the encouragement and stimulation that worshiping together provides, and because it pleases God (Hebrews 10:23–25).

John 4:23 reveals that the Father seeks people who will worship Him in spirit and in truth. That thought should motivate me to be present and to give my best effort whenever the church assembles for that purpose.

Points To Remember

- ◆ Power can result in presumption.
- ◆ Partial obedience is disobedience.
- ◆ Worship is God-centered, not man-centered.
- ◆ Worship is a command.

Points To Ponder

◆ *Satan doesn't care what we worship, as long as we don't worship God.*

◆ *Too many are trying to get something out of worship without putting anything into it.*

◆ *In genuine worship, a man pours out his heart, his mind, and his spirit as a sacrifice upon the altar of praise.*[3]

◆ *Worship is holy ground; and those who would worship God today must approach Him with no less reverence and awe than Moses did on Mt. Horeb.*[4]

◆ *"God is greatly to be feared in the assembly of the saints, and to be held in reverence by all those around Him" (Psalm 89:7).*

---

3. Jimmy Jividen, *Worship in Song* (Ft. Worth: Star Bible Publication, 1987), 19.
4. Dan Chambers, *Showtime: Worship in the Age of Show Business* (Nashville: 21st Century Christian, 1997), 48.

6

For Such a Time As This?

Grandmother, Mary Ella Hardeman Porch

Our *Declaration of Independence* claimed support from
"a firm reliance on the protection of divine providence."
May we never forget that we are, indeed, a nation under God.

*"Choose for yourselves today
whom you will serve."*

Joshua 24:15

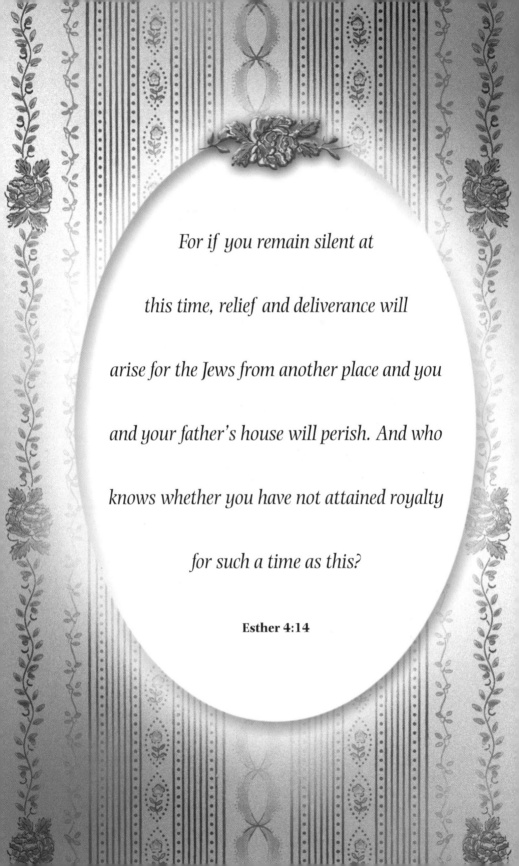

For if you remain silent at

this time, relief and deliverance will

arise for the Jews from another place and you

and your father's house will perish. And who

knows whether you have not attained royalty

for such a time as this?

Esther 4:14

For Such a Time as This?

A Lesson on Providence

Esther 4:1–17

David: The Man after God's Own Heart

A House for God

After the death of Saul, God removed the rule from his family and placed David, at the age of thirty, upon the throne as Israel's second king. During his forty-year reign he became the most beloved of all the Israelite kings; and despite some grave transgressions he had a contrite heart which led Jehovah to bless him.

David was a warrior, and during his tenure the kingdom of Israel grew rapidly. He ruled seven and one-half years in Hebron before capturing the stronghold of Zion and making it his capital. This ancient city, called Salem in Abraham's day, was known as Jerusalem when the new king renamed it the city of David, building himself a house there befitting of his position (2 Samuel 5:1–9).

In time, when he had put down all his enemies, David got it in his mind to build a permanent temple in which to place the ark of the covenant. He reasoned that it was not proper for him to be living in a luxurious house of cedar while the ark remained in its simple tabernacle (2 Samuel 7:2). Although David's intention was honorable, he, like Saul, was on the verge of presumption; and in reality it was condescending to God. David realized his mistake when Jehovah sent him a message that dripped with irony.

Through the prophet, God asked, "Are you the one who should build Me a house to dwell in?" (2 Samuel 7:5). He went on to say that David had the shoe on the wrong foot, so to speak. God did not need a temple because, as Paul explained in Acts 17:24–25, the Lord of Heaven and earth "does not dwell in temples made with hands; neither is He served by human hands, as though He needs anything, since He Himself gives to all life and breath and all things." Rather, it was He, Jehovah, the One who had taken David out of the pasture and made him ruler, who intended to build a house for David, a throne that would be established forever (2 Samuel 7:8).

Having said that, God was going to allow David's son Solomon to construct a permanent house of worship, so David contented himself with passing on all the plans and materials he had assembled (1 Chronicles 28). David's role was to

pave the way for the building of the temple, much like John the Baptist would pave the way for the building of the Lord's church, its antitype.

Apostasy

At David's death Solomon commenced his own forty-year reign in Jerusalem. He expanded the borders of Israel to their greatest extent and made his capital a fabulously rich and beautiful city where he received a steady stream of foreign diplomats bearing offerings of silver and gold, clothing, armor, spices, horses, mules, and other gifts. Silver in Jerusalem became so commonplace that it was nothing to Solomon, whose palace was furnished with vessels made only of gold (1 Kings 10:21–27). Such a lavish lifestyle drained the populace and led them to rebel after his death.

Although he showed great promise as a young man, Solomon further illustrates the adage: Power corrupts. He secured his political ties with a harem of foreign women that numbered seven hundred wives and three hundred concubines, and they turned away his heart from God. He built high places for their idols and did evil in the sight of Jehovah. At his death, the people were more than ready for a change. Unfortunately, idolatry had a foothold in the nation, and the people continued to sink deeper and deeper in its quagmire.

A Divided Kingdom

At Solomon's death, his son Rehoboam undertook to fill his shoes but immediately faced an ultimatum from the people. "Lower our taxes, and we will serve you as we did your father," they said. His senior counselors advised him to listen to their demand. (After all, what politician has ever been successful with a pledge of higher taxes?) But Rehoboam countered with a brash threat, saying, in essence, "If you think my father was hard on you, well, I'll be harder" (1 Kings 12:10 LB). The people's chief negotiator was Jeroboam, an appointee of King Solomon.

When Jeroboam saw that Rehoboam had lost the people's support, he became king over ten of the tribes of Israel. Judah, and a part of the tribe of Benjamin, remained loyal to the house of David. Rehoboam would have gone to war to preserve the union, but God restrained him saying, "This thing has come from Me" (1 Kings 12:24). As a result, the nation split into two separate kingdoms: Israel and Judah.

At this point we should note that God, who is omnipotent (all-powerful), omniscient (all-knowing), and omnipresent (not limited by space or time), saw all of these events in His mind's eye before they happened and used them in fulfilling His plans. This is called providence, a term derived from the Latin *providentia*, meaning "foresight." It is defined by McClintock and Strong as "the wisdom and power which God continually exercises in the preservation and government of the world, for the ends which He proposes to accomplish."[1]

Jeroboam, who was shrewd, realized that his position as king was tenuous. He reasoned that the tribes would likely talk about reuniting if the people returned to Jerusalem to keep the appointed feasts. So he established a counterfeit religion at Dan and Bethel with two golden calves, saying, "It is too much for you to go up to Jerusalem; behold your gods, O Israel, that brought you up from the land of Egypt" (1 Kings 12:28). His action was so reprehensible to God that all the corrupt kings who followed were said to cling "to the sins of Jeroboam the son of Nebat, which he made Israel sin" (2 Kings 3:3).

Exile

Jeroboam was the first of nineteen Israelite monarchs who ruled from 931 to 722 B.C. They represented nine different dynasties because so many were ousted from office by assassination. Not one of them left an honorable legacy. The last to reign was Hoshea, who was better than some of his predecessors; but the nation had gone so far in violence, immorality, and idolatry that they were past all redemption.

Before they entered Canaan, God placed before Israel blessings and curses, assuring them of prosperity if they would obey Him, but warning that unfaithfulness would bring captivity in a foreign land (Deuteronomy 28:62–64). When He sent prophets to correct their wandering ways, the people persecuted them instead of listening (Matthew 5:11–12). It appears they were cut from the same cloth as their ancestors, to whom Moses had said, "You have been rebellious against the Lord from the day that I knew you" (Deuteronomy 9:24).

In 726 B.C. the Assyrian king Shalmaneser made Israel his tributary. After a while King Hoshea, tired of being taxed, formed a secret alliance with the king of Egypt, which angered the Assyrians. They laid siege to Israel's capital at Samaria for three years until the city surrendered, and they carried its people into exile in 722 B.C.

---

1. Wayne Jackson, Freed-Hardeman University Lectures (Henderson, TN, 1997).

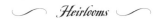

Captivity

In the south the tribe of Judah, plus the legitimate priests and other faithful who had emigrated from Israel (2 Chronicles 11:13–14), fared only a little better. They, too, had nineteen kings, all descendants of David. Six or eight were fairly decent kings, but overall Judah followed in the same sins as Israel.

In 606 B.C. Nebuchadnezzar, the crown prince of Babylon began a series of attacks on Jerusalem that continued for approximately twenty years. (Nebuchadnezzar became king shortly after the first attack against Jerusalem.) Each attack resulted in captives being carried off and valuables looted from the city. In 586 B.C. King Nebuchadnezzar deported the last of the people, except for the very poorest, and destroyed the city of Jerusalem by fire.

In captivity the hearts of the Israelites turned once again to the God of their fathers. Through the prophet Jeremiah, God urged them to live at peace in the land, promising that in time He would certainly return them to their homeland (Jeremiah 25:11–12; 29:10). Babylon was conquered by the Medo-Persian Empire under the reign of Darius the Mede and Cyrus the Persian in 538 B.C. True to His word, God moved Cyrus to restore His people to Jerusalem. Amazingly, Isaiah had written 150 years beforehand that one Cyrus, the shepherd of Jehovah, would rebuild Jerusalem and the temple (Isaiah 44:28).

The scribe records in 2 Chronicles 36:22–23 that the Lord stirred up the spirit of Cyrus to allow the Jews' return, although Cyrus did not understand that Jehovah was using him (Isaiah 45:1–4). God was providentially employing this foreign king to further His plan for the Jewish nation and for all mankind.

From Orphan to Royalty

No clearer illustration of God's providence can be found than in the life of Esther, whose story is recorded near the end of the books of history. When many of the Jews were returning under Cyrus to the land of their nativity, some who had made new lives in Chaldea (Babylonia) chose to remain there. Among them were a Jewish girl named Hadassah (Esther) and her kinsman-guardian Mordecai.

The Babylonian Empire was under the reign of Xerxes, or Ahasuerus, the son of Darius I. The king had deposed his wife Vashti and was looking for a new queen to take her place. When he assembled a bevy of beautiful young virgins to vie for the honor, Esther was among those brought to the palace. Although she did not seek to stand out from the others, it was she whom the king favored and chose to be his queen (Esther 2:12–16).

During this time, Mordecai was working in some official capacity in the king's gate. There he chanced to overhear a plot against the life of King Ahasuerus and reported it. His heroism was recorded in the official chronicles but promptly forgotten.

A new threat arose to all Jews throughout the empire from a proud and arrogant prince named Haman. The prince developed an intense dislike for Mordecai, whose convictions would not allow him to bow to any man. Haman, unmoved by Mordecai's piety, resolved to put the Jew to death. His diabolical plan was to persuade the king that all Jews—the name then used for the children of Israel—were a threat to national security. Ahasuerus, not knowing that Esther was Jewish, was persuaded to write it into law.

All over the empire the Jews went into mourning while Mordecai enlisted the queen's help. He asked that she petition Ahasuerus for her own life and the lives of her people. Mordecai, no doubt a man of faith, was confident they would prevail, with Esther as the means of their delivery. He reasoned with her, "Who knows whether you have not attained royalty for such a time as this?" (Esther 4:14).

From Fasting to Feasting

Esther and her people fasted three days before she undertook a daring plan. She entertained the king and the proud Haman, who was so flattered that he immediately constructed a gallows for Mordecai. Haman was confident that his plan would soon come together. To paraphrase the poet, however, "The best-laid plans of mice and men often go awry." Haman's plans began to unravel when the king, struck with insomnia, called for the official records. Strangely enough, he discovered that very night that he had never rewarded Mordecai's heroism and determined immediately to right the wrong.

Meanwhile, Esther prepared a second banquet for the king and Haman, where she unexpectedly revealed Haman's wicked plot. When Ahasuerus found Haman begging for the queen's mercy, he took it as an assault upon her and immediately imposed the death sentence upon him.

By law the king could not rescind his previous command, but he encouraged all those with any political influence to ally themselves with the Jews. As a result, they defended themselves from all their enemies and survived. The Jews celebrated their deliverance with a feast which is still observed annually as the Feast of Purim. Although God's name is mentioned nowhere in the account of Esther, the message of His providence pervades the book.

Is God at work in my life?

God works today through providence.

Some people have the philosophy that "whatever will be, will be." They never consider that a higher power controls our universe. We can see that power at work in the maintenance of natural laws. God also works in the lives of His people to bring about His purposes (Philippians 2:13).

The Scriptures attest to the fact that many things happen randomly in our

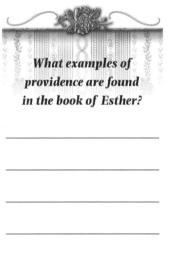

What examples of providence are found in the book of Esther?

_____

_____

_____

_____

_____

lives. Solomon wrote that "time and chance happen to them all" (Ecclesiastes 9:11 NKJV). Jesus Himself, in telling the parable of the good Samaritan, said, "By chance there came down a certain priest that way" (Luke 10:31 KJV). But we must not assume that God never works providentially in our lives today as He did in the past.

One's view of providence is determined by his understanding of God. The atheist, for example, does not believe in providence because he denies that God exists. The deist, who believes that God created the world, nevertheless denies that He guides it or intervenes in any way with its course of destiny. Therefore, he does not accept the role of providence, either. The Bible, however, teaches that God both created the world and continues to operate in it. He has an eternal foreknowledge of events that will happen (Acts 2:23; 1 Peter 1:2) and has predestined certain things to occur, that is, that good will ultimately triumph over evil and that the redeemed in Christ will be saved (Genesis 3:15; Ephesians 1:4–6). God is also aware of what is happening, even to the most minute detail (Matthew 10:29–30), and He is attentive to the needs and prayers of the righteous (John 9:31; 1 Peter 3:12). His providence means that He is in control of the world and that He provides the means to accomplish His purposes on the earth. William Cowper said, "God moves in a mysterious way His wonders to perform."

God allows me freedom of choice.

God can use individuals who oppose Him. We noted this in the example of Pharaoh. Romans 9:17 states that God raised him up to show His power and to declare His name in all the earth. The king was still accountable for his actions, because all men are agents of free choice (Acts 10:34–35). Remember Joshua's charge to the Israelites: "Choose for your-selves today whom you will serve"? (Joshua 24:15). God might even use entire nations which oppose Him, just as He employed the Babylonian Empire to bring Israel to its knees (Habakkuk 1:5–6).

What does Proverbs 1:28–29 teach about free choice?

_____

_____

_____

_____

_____

God's providence transcends the age of miracles.

Throughout history, God has sometimes used miracles to accomplish His purposes. Often they were used to confirm His choice of individuals in various roles, as in the case of Abraham, Sarah, and Moses, whom we have studied. He brought the plagues upon Egypt as a judgment against that nation, but those signs and wonders also confirmed His power to the Israelites.

Jesus' life began with a miracle, and throughout His ministry He used mir-acles to confirm the fact that He was God's Son. The Gospel writers left a record of more than thirty miracles performed by Jesus. John writes that many other signs were performed by the Lord in the presence of the disciples which were not even recorded, adding "but these have been written that you may believe that Jesus is the Christ, the Son of God" (John 20:30–31). There is no evidence that He ever used His power for any personal gain (Luke 4).

How is the word miracle *commonly misused?*

The apostles also had the power to work "signs and wonders and miracles" as a means of confirm-ing the message they taught (2 Corinthians 12:12). About the time that their writings were being com-piled into the New Testament canon, the signs ceased (1 Corinthians 13:9–10). Since the function of mira-cles was to produce faith, they became unnecessary

_____

_____

_____

_____

_____

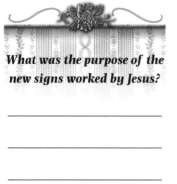

What was the purpose of the new signs worked by Jesus?

_____

_____

_____

for our day because we have the completed Scriptures, which testify to the divinity of Jesus.

The Christ Himself said, "Blessed are they who did not see, and yet believed" (John 20:29). Our walk is by faith rather than sight (2 Corinthians 5:7); it is based upon the testimony of the Holy Spirit rather than miraculous signs. Incidentally, Jesus taught in Luke 16:29–31 that those who have no faith in the Scriptures would not believe even if a miracle were performed for them.

This is not to say that God is not at work in today's world. He certainly continues to work providentially, and His methods are no less marvelous when He works through His natural laws rather than outside them. God's providence is ongoing, despite the fact that miraculous signs have ceased.

God's providence is unfathomable.

When we pray, "Thy will be done," we confess that God's ways transcend our ability to comprehend them. We trust in the promise of Romans 8:28 that all things work together for good to those who love God and are called according-

David wrote that God's mercy and faithfulness extend to the heavens and into the clouds (Psalm 36:5). How does this give comfort?

_____

_____

_____

ing to His purpose. And we have confidence that God does indeed hear the prayers of the righteous, although His answers are not always obvious (Proverbs 15:29).

Paul prayed three times for God to remove his thorn in the flesh. Whatever the problem, God chose not to remove it, saying, "My grace is sufficient for you." Paul came to understand that his thorn served to keep him humble because he had been privy to special visions and revelations from God (2 Corinthians 12:1–9).

The founding fathers of America believed they were following the direction of divine providence. John Adams viewed the settlement of this nation with reverence and wonder, "as the opening of a grand scene and design in providence."[2] Likewise, our *Declaration of Independence* claimed support from

---

2. John Adams, Notes for "A Dissertation on the Canon and Feudal Law," 1765.

"a firm reliance on the protection of divine providence." May we never forget that we are, indeed, a nation under God.

We can only concur with Paul, who said of God's providence, "Oh, the depth of the riches both of the wisdom and knowledge of God! How unsearchable are His judgments and unfathomable His ways!" (Romans 11:33).

Points To Remember

- God works today through providence.
- God allows me freedom of choice.
- God's providence transcends the age of miracles.
- God's providence is unfathomable.

Points To Ponder

- *Do not be afraid to trust an unknown future to a known God.*
- *It's pretty hard for the Lord to guide a man if he hasn't made up his mind which way he wants to go.*
- *When we let God guide, He will provide.*
- *God calls for us to stand, though not always to understand.*
- *Luck is what happens when preparation meets opportunity.*

Shall We Not Accept Adversity?

Great-grandfather, Dr. John B. Hardeman

In reality, life is absolutely fair. God has given humans freedom
in exchange for responsibility. Abuse of our freedom has created
pain for everyone, even the innocent.

*"The greatest part of our happiness and misery depends
on our dispositions and not on our circumstances."*

Martha Washington

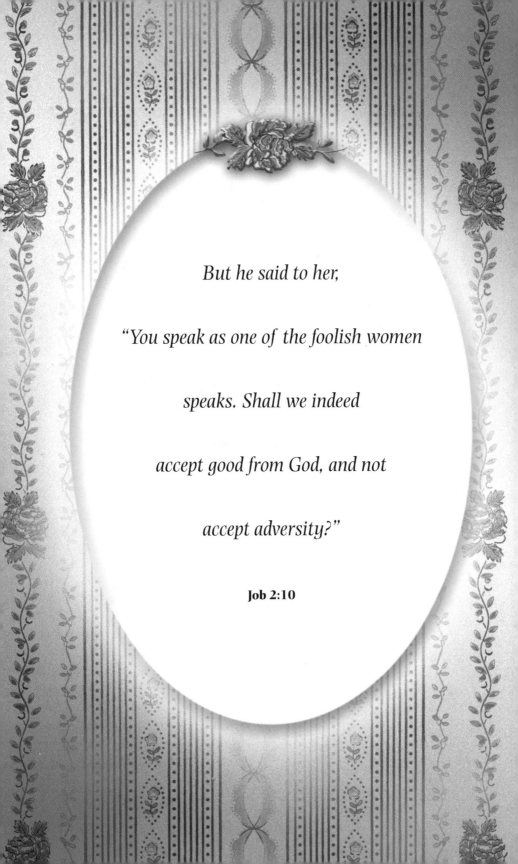

But he said to her,

"You speak as one of the foolish women

speaks. Shall we indeed

accept good from God, and not

accept adversity?"

Job 2:10

Shall We Not Accept Adversity?

A Lesson on Suffering

Job 1:1–2:13

Lessons from the Books of Wisdom

The Books of Poetry

The first seventeen books of the Old Testament consist of five books of the law and twelve books of history. The third Old Testament division is a section of poetry and prose called Wisdom Literature. It includes the books of Job, Psalms, Proverbs, Ecclesiastes, and Song of Solomon.

Hebrew poetry, unlike English, contains no rhyming words. It is made up of ideas arranged in a form known as parallelism. Two lines back to back might express the same idea in different words, or they might state contrasting ideas. The book of Job is a poetic drama, in which the main characters deal with the universal problem of suffering. Job's question, "Shall we indeed accept good from God and not accept adversity?" is one with which people have wrestled for generations.

No one knows the author of Job or the time of its writing, but many scholars believe that the book is one of the earliest in the Old Testament. Job was the head of a large family, and he offered sacrifices for them in the manner of the early patriarchs (Job 1:5). The narrative reveals that Job lived to be quite old (Job 42:16), well advanced of the seventy years that was common by the time of Psalm 90:10, though there were exceptions to the rule.

Good Versus Evil

The book begins, "There was a man in the land of Uz, whose name was Job." We discover that he was a man of remarkable wealth and prominence who was married and the father of ten children. Job owned thousands of head of livestock, including sheep, camels, oxen, and donkeys; and his large estate was managed by a number of servants. So that we might fully appreciate his stature, the author informs us that Job was the greatest of the sons of the East.

Most significantly, he was a godly man who didn't let his wealth go to his head. He was morally upright, no small accomplishment for one who moved among the rich and famous. He treated his servants fairly and practiced benevolence toward the needy, the widows, and the orphans, according to chapter 31. (Already we find ourselves admiring such a man!) Ezekiel placed him in the

company of Noah and Daniel as one of the most outstanding citizens of history (Ezekiel 14:14). No human accolade, however, compared to the fact that, to God, he was "My servant, Job."

Our Adversary

Chapters 1 and 2 tell the story of a great challenge between God and the adversary of man, who is here called Satan. Elsewhere the Bible refers to him as the devil (Matthew 4:1), the evil one (Matthew 13:19), a murderer and a liar (John 8:44).

My friend Doug Couch, a biologist as well as a minister of the gospel, notes that Satan appears appropriately as a snake in the Genesis account. Deadly snakes kill their prey by constriction or with venom, and Satan is adept at both methods. Matthew 13:22 tells us that he has the power to choke his victims with temptation and adversity, and he is also a master of the venomous lie (Genesis 3:4).

According to Mark 3:22, Satan is Beelzebub, the ruler of demons. We know that he is God's enemy (Matthew 13:38–43). Unlike the demonic beings whom God has confined to pits of darkness until the judgment (2 Peter 2:4; Jude 6), Satan himself is not restricted; and our first glimpse of him in the first chapter of Job occurs after he has been "roaming about on the earth and walking around on it" (Job 1:7; 1 Peter 5:8). He shows up among the sons of God—angelic beings, Job 38:7—on a day when they come to present themselves before Him.

Satan's Confrontation with God

God's encounter with Satan began with a question: "Have you considered My servant Job? For there is no one like him on the earth, a blameless and upright man, fearing God and turning away from evil." It brought a swift insult from the devil. In essence, he asked, "Why shouldn't he, when you pay him so well? You have always protected him and his home and his property from all harm. You have prospered everything he does—look how rich he is! No wonder he worships you!" (Job 1:9–10 LB). He implied, and not very subtly, that God is unworthy of true worship and that only those who hope to gain something from Him bother to worship Him.

Satan then issued a challenge. "Let me tear down the protective hedge you have placed around him and Job will curse you to your face" (LB). Surprisingly,

God agreed to the proposition, with the one condition that Satan not harm Job himself (Job 1:12).

The Test

Almost immediately a series of tragic events befell Job which remind us of the adage: When it rains, it pours! Using wicked men and natural disasters, Satan wiped out everything Job had; and as if this were not enough, all ten of his children died when a violent windstorm hit the house where they were gathered. In one day, Job went from prosperous to impoverished.

What seems especially tortuous is that the news of all these catastrophes came in waves, so that he no sooner finished reeling from one shock until there was another. When he heard about the deaths of his children, Job tore his robe and shaved his head according to the custom of his day. He then prostrated himself in worship as he uttered these words, "Naked I came from my mother's womb, and naked I shall return there. The Lord gave and the Lord has taken away. Blessed be the name of the Lord" (Job 1:21).

Although he had no idea why these things had happened, Job did not sin by blaming God, as the devil had predicted (Job 1:22). Not to be outdone, however, Satan taunted, "Skin for skin! Yes, all that a man has he will give for his life. However, put forth Thy hand, now, and touch his bone and his flesh; he will curse Thee to Thy face" (Job 2:4–5). In other words, Satan suggests, Job is just trying to protect himself. He is pretending to worship God in hopes that his own skin will be spared. And the Lord answered, "Behold, he is in your power, only spare his life" (Job 2:6).

The account leaves no doubt that Satan is powerful, "the god of this world" according to 2 Corinthians 4:4. Even Michael the archangel refused to bring a railing accusation against him, calling instead for the Lord's rebuke (Jude 9). I recently noted some young people at a church gathering wearing shirts that said, "Satan, bring it on!" Their resolve is admirable, but there is wisdom in the ancient proverb which says that he who eats with the devil needs a long spoon. God tells us to resist the devil while giving him no opportunity to attack (James 4:7; Ephesians 4:27).

Did God care that Job was suffering? Of course He cared! God gave His offspring the freedom to make choices, knowing that it would bring sin into the world and ultimately necessitate the death of His Son. "For God so loved the world" is a truth too high for human comprehension!

Job's Affliction

Then Satan afflicted Job with sore boils "from the sole of his foot to the crown of his head." Although his disease goes unnamed, we learn about its side-effects throughout the book. Among them were itching (Job 2:8), decreased appetite (3:24), depression (3:25), running sores (7:5), bad breath (19:17), darkened eyes (16:16), weight loss (19:20), pain (30:17), and fever (30:30).[1] The poor man was in so much torment that the only relief he could find was in scraping himself with a piece of broken pottery!

He sorely needed comfort from those who cared. Grace Noll Crowell has written the following:

> Let me come in where you are weeping, friend,
>   And let me take your hand.
> I, who have known a sorrow such as yours,
>   Can understand.
>
> Let me come in—I would be very still
>   Beside you in your grief;
> I would not bid you cease your weeping, friend,
>   Tears bring relief.
>
> Let me come in—I would only breathe a prayer,
>   And hold your hand,
> For I have known a sorrow such as yours,
>   And understand.[2]

Euripides wrote that a man's best possession is a sympathetic wife. Job's wife asked him bitterly, "Do you still hold fast your integrity? Curse God and die!" We should consider that she was hurting also, having lost her children, her security, and in a sense her husband as well. But she was not sympathetic. Chrysostom posed the question of why the devil left Job's wife when he took his children. He concludes, "Because he thought her a good scourge, by which to plague him more acutely than by any other means."[3]

Job reprimanded his wife for speaking like a foolish woman: "Shall we indeed accept good from God and not accept adversity?" Whatever questions were tormenting Job's mind, he kept them to himself until he could sort

---

1. Wayne Jackson, *The Book of Job* (Abilene: Quality Publications, 1983), 22.
2. Grace Noll Crowell, "To One in Sorrow," in *Tapestries of Life* (Carmel, NY: Guideposts, 1974), 219.
3. C. F. Keil and F. Delitzsch, *Commentary on the Old Testament*, vol. 4 (Grand Rapids: Eerdmans, 1978), 72.

through them so that with his lips he did not sin. As his suffering intensified, his struggle to understand why led him to challenge God. In the next chapter we look at Job's attempt to reconcile his pain with God's goodness.

Who, Me?

Shall I have to suffer also?

Suffering does not originate with God.

Suffering is a part of the human experience, and in the words of one ancient, "He who learns must suffer." According to Proverbs 13, life is hard for one who lives in sin because he reaps the consequences of his lifestyle. Godly people, however, also experience a share of suffering, and sometimes it is because of their faithfulness (2 Timothy 3:12). Solomon noted that weeping is as much a part of life as laughing (Ecclesiastes 3:4), and Shakespeare concurred, noting that "sorrow breaks the seasons." We can count on it.

The atheist argues that human misery proves there is no God. How, he asks, could God subject His creation to suffering and still be good? Job himself continued to struggle with this question at one point, as his tortured mind probed why he was being punished. In Job 9:22 he accused God of destroying both the guiltless and the wicked. He even went so far as to charge God with mocking the despair of the innocent. He could not understand why God would allow terrible things to happen to him since he was trying to live a good life. Job's feeling was, "It isn't fair!"

Parents hear this refrain often from their children. Maybe we replied on occasion, "Life isn't always fair." In reality, life is absolutely fair. God has given humans freedom in exchange for responsibility. The abuse of our freedom has created pain for everyone, even the innocent. Jesus Himself, although sinless, was not immune to it. So Job became a victim of life in this very real world where storms strike, wicked people commit violence, and sickness and disease strike indiscriminately. All of these things happen because we are free to make personal choices.

Martha Washington once said, "The greatest part of our happiness and misery depends on our dispositions and not on our circumstances." It is the clouds in life which often produce showers of blessing that we want and need.

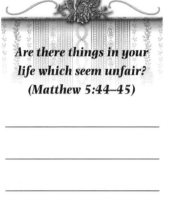

Are there things in your life which seem unfair?
(Matthew 5:44–45)

_____

_____

_____

_____

How did Jesus endure the suffering he had to undergo?
(Hebrews 12:2)

_____

_____

_____

_____

Although suffering is unavoidable, we recognize that good can come from it.

Suffering can draw us closer to God.

Some of the greatest blessings in life are born out of pain. Childbirth is a good example. No pain is so quickly forgotten as that of a mother in labor, because it ushers in such joy and happiness. Sometimes suffering is the vehicle by which something good comes into our lives.

There is an old story of a lone shipwreck survivor cast upon an uninhabited island. He built a hut and stored within it what he could salvage from his burning ship. Every day he scanned the ocean and prayed that someone would rescue him. One day, returning from a hunt, he saw with horror that his belongings were going up in smoke. The man was devastated until the next day when a ship arrived and the captain told him, "I saw your smoke signal."[4] His misfortune was really a blessing in disguise!

Someone has said that the most comforting phrase in Scripture is, "It came to pass." Romans 8:28 assures us that difficulties do work together for our good when we are called according to God's purpose; but it doesn't happen overnight. Hardships afford a reality check as to our utter dependence upon God and often drive us to the Bible for comfort. Psalm 119:71 states, "It is good for me that I was afflicted, that I may learn Thy statutes."

Suffering enables us to sympathize with others.

There are times when we sit with a friend who is despondent and we want to say, "I know how you feel." But unless we have been there we probably don't. Through suffering we learn how to empathize with others.

My mother suffered from a series of illnesses which left her immobile, in pain, and suffering from dementia. She spent the last year of her life in a nurs-

---

4. A. L. Franks, ed., *Magnolia Messenger* (Kosciusko, MS).

ing home, which was deeply painful for our family. Later, when a friend was in a similar situation, I really could say, "I understand what you are going through." Robert Browning Hamilton summed up the sentiment with these words:

> I walked a mile with Pleasure
> She chattered all the way,
> But left me none the wiser
> For all she had to say.
>
> I walked a mile with Sorrow,
> And ne'er a word said she,
> But, oh, the things I learned from her
> When Sorrow walked with me!

As God comforts us in our afflictions, what does He desire of us?
(2 Corinthians 1:3–4)

_____

_____

_____

_____

Suffering can change our perspective.

While the Scriptures command that we "weep with those who weep" (Romans 12:15), people who practice self-pity never seem to get enough sympathy and must throw their own pity-parties. One shut-in regularly berated all her visitors, and as a result they stopped coming at all. Other people seem to handle their misfortunes with such grace and gratitude that they draw others to them.

There is a fictitious story of a young man who was at the end of his rope. He dropped to his knees and prayed, "Lord, I can't go on. My cross is too heavy to bear." He was told that he could exchange his cross, if he liked, for another. The young man was relieved, and upon entering a large room he saw many crosses, some so tall that the tops were not visible. But he spotted a tiny cross leaning against a far wall, and he whispered, "I like that one, Lord." The Lord replied, "My son, that is the cross you just brought in."[5] The story illustrates that there is nothing like adversity to make us aware of how blessed we have been and how much we have taken for granted.

Christianity seemed to spread most rapidly when persecution was the strongest. Paul's personal hardships sharpened his focus on Heaven and prompted him to write, "The sufferings of this present time are not worthy to be compared with the glory that is to be revealed to us" (Romans 8:18). James

---

5. A. L. Franks, ed., *Magnolia Messenger*.

urged Christians to "consider it all joy . . . when you encounter various trials, knowing that the testing of your faith produces endurance" (James 1:2–3). None of us welcomes the difficult times in our lives, but if we look we will find a blessing somewhere within them. There is no dark cloud which Satan can send into our lives from which God cannot release a shower of blessing.

Points To Remember

◆ Suffering does not originate with God.

◆ Suffering can draw us closer to God.

◆ Suffering enables us to sympathize with others.

◆ Suffering can change our perspective.

Points To Ponder

◆ *Many people expect to get to the promised land without going through the wilderness.*

◆ *All the fertile lands are down in the valley.*

◆ *"Character cannot be developed in ease and quiet. Only through experience of trial and suffering can the soul be strengthened, ambition inspired, and success achieved." Helen Keller*

◆ *The difficulties of life are intended to make us better—not bitter.*

If a Man Dies, Will He Live Again?

Great-great-grandparents, William B. and Matilda Porch

"Lord, make me to know my end, and what is the extent of my days, let me know how transient I am. Behold, Thou hast made my days as hand-breaths, and my lifetime as nothing in Thy sight, surely every man at his best is a mere breath. Surely every man walks about as a phantom."

Psalm 39:4-6

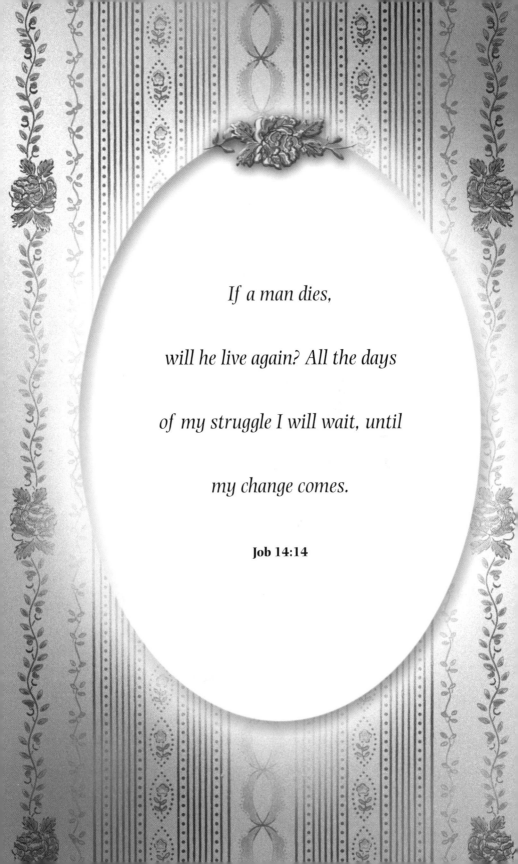

If a man dies,

will he live again? All the days

of my struggle I will wait, until

my change comes.

Job 14:14

If a Man Dies, Will He Live Again?

A Lesson on Immortality

Job 14:1–22

Facing Death: The Ultimate Test

A Great Man Falls

I vividly recall the day my college friends and I heard the news of President John F. Kennedy's assassination. There was a sense of shock and disbelief that one so famous should be as vulnerable as everyone else. Since Job, too, was a great man, the report of his misfortunes must have stunned those who heard it.

When Job's friends learned of his devastation, three of them made plans together to go and see how he was doing. Eliphaz is often assumed to be the eldest, and he always speaks first. He was from Teman, located in Edom according to Obadiah 1:8–9, and he may have been among Esau's kin (Genesis 36:11, 15). He was accompanied by Bildad, a Shuhite who was possibly a descendant of Abraham (Genesis 25:2), and Zophar, a Naamathite. They met and traveled together to Job's home in the land of Uz.

The three men were unprepared for the sight of their old friend. Even from a distance the pitiful figure sitting on the ground moved them beyond words. They tore their robes and threw dust over their heads in customary gestures of grief, while they sat with Job for a week without conversing.

The visitors were genuinely distressed by his plight. They wept, and throughout the week, while Job was gathering his thoughts into some order, each of them struggled to put together the pieces of his calamity. What could it mean? They grew increasingly suspicious that Job was guilty of a great and hidden wickedness for which he was being punished.

Miserable Comforters

People deal with grief in various ways. Sometimes there is disbelief and even anger before reality sets in. Once Job broke his silence, his words erupted in an outburst of emotion. He cursed the day of his birth; in other words, he wished he had never been born (Job 3:3). Why, he asked, couldn't I have died at birth? Why must I keep on living? (Job 3:11). He wondered, "Why is light given to him who suffers, and life to the bitter of soul, who long for death, but there is none?" (Job 3:20–21).

The elder Eliphaz interrupted Job's lament by asking rather politely if he might say something without upsetting him. He proceeded to counsel Job that suffering is God's way of getting man's attention when he has done something wrong. He pleaded for Job to make things right with God, saying, "Do not despise the discipline of the Almighty" (Job 5:17). He suggested that if Job would repent, God might be inclined to turn things around for him.

Eliphaz probably meant well, but his advice stung like salt in Job's wounds. The patriarch lashed back at his friends for being "miserable comforters." He chastised them for being so quick to pass judgment on him when they had not even tried to offer him any help (Job 6:14–18). He challenged them also to show what he had done if he were such a sinner. Job prayed with the most pitiful pleas that God would end his suffering, saying, "Would that God were willing to crush me; that He would loose His hand and cut me off!" (Job 6:9).

Bildad was annoyed by Job's lamentation, and being less tactful than Eliphaz, he very bluntly suggested that Job's children may have died because of their wrongdoing (Job 8:4). It was a horrible charge, especially since it had no merit whatsoever! Although his statement was the epitome of insensitivity, Bildad seemed to think that he must say something to move Job to repentance. What a lesson for us when we attempt to give advice without the facts (James 1:19). Bildad also lectured that "God will not reject a man of integrity" (Job 8:20), an unsubtle accusation against Job's character. With friends like these, Satan had no need to afflict Job with any further enemies!

Dealing with Depression

When Zophar concurred with the others as to Job's guilt, the patriarch became more depressed and consumed with morbid thoughts. He brooded over the brevity of life and wondered why it even mattered. He came to the conclusion that "man, who is born of woman, is short-lived and full of turmoil, like a flower that comes forth and withers" (Job 14:1–2). He complained that man lives out his short life like a hired man and pleaded with God to take His gaze off him long enough for him to get a little rest (Job 14:6). His words were terribly cynical, and they do not sound like the words of a patient man. When James 5:11 speaks of the patience of Job, he is discussing his perseverance. Job certainly did complain, long and hard. Yet he never cursed God; and although he often felt that he would be better off dead, he found the strength to continue.

While his mind was torn between hope and despair, Job expressed the wish that God would hide him in the grave. He wondered, "If a man dies, will he live again?" In his heart, he believed he would, for he continued, "All the days of my struggle I will wait, until my change comes. Thou wilt call, and I will answer Thee; Thou wilt long for the work of Thy hands" (Job 14:14–15).

Sadly, Job had allowed negative people to make him doubt God's love for him. He thought God had cast him off, and that pained him more than all his losses. He longed for the day when God would look favorably on him again.

Hope: "My Redeemer Lives"

In a second round of accusations, the three visitors warned Job that worse things would happen if he persisted in claiming innocence, but he could take no more of their charges (Job 15:17–25). He told them, "My spirit is broken, my days are extinguished, the grave is ready for me" (Job 17:1). Mentally, he could see them laying his body to rest in the ground, among the worms. Yet, in a flash of prophetic insight, Job said:

> I know that my Redeemer lives, and at the last He will take His stand on the earth. Even after my skin is destroyed, yet from my flesh I shall see God; whom I myself shall behold, and whom my eyes shall see and not another. My heart faints within me (Job 19:25–27).

The word *redeemer* comes from a Hebrew root for the next of kin whose duty it was to buy back, deliver, or avenge a relative.[1] Job was longing for someone to take his side and plead his case before God. He did not know, as we do, that there is a mediator between God and man, "the man Christ Jesus" (1 Timothy 2:5). (How thankful we are to live in an age when we can hold that hope with assurance!) Still, Job believed that he would see God someday and that he would be able to talk to Him face to face. We agree with Job that such a magnificent thought is enough to make the heart faint!

Tempted and Tried

Not yet finished, the three men brought specific charges against Job which were totally unsubstantiated. They painted him as a man devoid of human kindness, one who had cruelly withheld relief from the hungry and those in need (Job 22). Job denied it, and reminded them of the sterling reputation he had enjoyed (Job 31). He considered their accusations utterly unfair.

Job's friends had manufactured these charges because it was the only reasonable explanation they could imagine. They, and even Job himself, were oper-

---

1. James Strong, *The Exhaustive Concordance of the Bible* (Holman: Nashville, n.d.), 25.

ating under the assumption that the righteous are supposed to be rewarded and the wicked punished in this life. Yet Job had seen that often the opposite happens: the ungodly prosper while innocent people suffer without cause (Job 21). E. S. Lorenz made the same observation in the words of this hymn:

> Tempted and tried, we're oft made to wonder
>> Why it should be thus all the day long;
> While there are others living about us
>> Never molested though in the wrong.

Job found his theology at odds with reality, and that led him to question whether or not it is worthwhile to live a godly life (Job 35:3).

When a fourth visitor arrived, he showed himself, though young, to be a man of some insight by counseling the others that there was no evidence of any sin on Job's part. Elihu said that Job was wrong, however, to call God's justice into question. He even suggested to Job that God might be disciplining him for his good rather than punishing him (Job 33:29–30). He advised Job to accept his misfortune and get on with life rather than think about death (Job 36:20).

Before the patriarch could digest Elihu's advice, a whirlwind arose and Job got his wish. He had been arguing that he would love to speak with God face to face, but he was not prepared for that amazing opportunity. Job had been putting the Lord on trial, and now it was his turn to be interrogated. God challenged Job with question after question, none of which he could answer. The encounter gave the patriarch a new appreciation for God's sovereignty; and it altered his entire outlook on life. Job had not received one word of explanation as to why he was suffering, but He understood the one thing that matters—God controls this universe!

Submission: The Final Test

The circumstances of his life were unchanged, but Job was not. He deeply regretted his accusations against God and bowed his soul in submission. He determined to yield himself to the will of God, whatever that might be. It was then that the events in his life began to change. First, God required Job's friends to seek his forgiveness; and after, Job prayed for them, God began restoring his fortunes twofold. Note that Job's speeches reveal a great deal of anger, and forgiving his accusers was an important element in his grief recovery—quite possibly his final test. Finally, Job was reunited with all his kin and former friends who seem to have shunned him before (Job 42:11). In time he fathered ten more children who brought great happiness and purpose back into his life, and he died at last, "an old man and full of days."

Job must have been forever thankful that God had spared his life when he himself had grown weary of it. James applauds Job's endurance and reminds us that his story illustrates God's compassion and mercy (James 5:11). It convinces us that we, too, can find the strength to persevere in trying times, knowing that God is in control.

Will God be with me in death?

God cares for those who grieve.

According to Hebrews 9:27, everyone has an appointment with death. Solomon wrote that there is a time to be born, and a time to die and that the living know they will die (Ecclesiastes 3:2; 9:5). It was Benjamin Franklin who quipped that besides taxes, death is the only certainty in life.

When Job saw his own death approaching, he observed that his days were "swifter than a weaver's shuttle" (Job 7:6). "When a few years are past," he predicted, "I shall go the way of no return" (Job 16:22). Like Job, we realize as we age that life is indeed brief, and we appreciate the truth in these passages:

> Lord, make me to know my end, and what is the extent of my days, let me know how transient I am. Behold, Thou hast made my days as handbreadths, and my lifetime as nothing in Thy sight, surely every man at his best is a mere breath. Surely every man walks about as a phantom (Psalm 39:4–6).

> My days are like a lengthened shadow; and I wither away like grass (Psalm 102:11).

> As for man, his days are like grass; as a flower of the field, so he flourishes. When the wind has passed over it, it is no more; and its place acknowledges it no longer (Psalm 103:15–16).

> All flesh is grass, and all its loveliness is like the flower of the field. The grass withers, the flower fades, when the breath of the Lord blows upon it (Isaiah 40:6–7).

You are just a vapor that appears for a little while and then vanishes away (James 4:14).

We should remember that it was never God's desire for man to die. Death is the wage paid by Satan, contrary to what he told Eve (Romans 6:23); and for this reason the Scripture says that he is the father of lies (John 8:44). We can always assure those who are grieving that God cares, because He takes note of every death, even that of the sparrow which falls to the ground (Matthew 10:29).

One lesson from Job's friends is to be cautious about giving unwarranted advice. We should never tell anyone, for example, that God took a loved one because He needed him or her more in Heaven. Neither should we assume that God is chastening us by taking those we love.

The righteous are at peace in death.

Jesus talked about life after death. In Matthew 22:31–32 He said,

> But regarding the resurrection of the dead, have you not read that which was spoken to you by God, saying, 'I am the God of Abraham, and the God of Isaac, and the God of Jacob?' He is not the God of the dead but of the living.

Paul wrote that Jesus "abolished death, and brought life and immortality to light through the gospel" (2 Timothy 1:10).

When his suffering was most intense, Job viewed death as a place where the weary are at rest. Is there any more comforting word in the English language than rest? To the nation of Israel it was the promised land, symbolic of the true rest that awaits the faithful, according to Hebrews 4:9 and Revelation 14:13.

What thought did David find hard to fathom?
(Psalm 8:4)

In the Genesis account we saw how God made Adam of the dust and filled him with the breath of life; and he became a living soul (Genesis 2:7). Paul noted that we are spirit, soul, and body (1 Thessalonians 5:23). At death, a separation occurs when the spirit returns to God who gave it and the body returns to the dust from which it came (James 2:26; Ecclesiastes 12:7).

In a nearby cemetery, a young woman lies buried who died over a century ago. For years, her sweetheart kept a lantern burning near her grave, because he knew she feared the dark. That tender story is indicative of what many people believe, that the spirits of their loved ones rest within the grave. There, they believe, the soul sleeps peacefully—or not so peacefully!—until the day of the resurrection. The idea of soul sleeping prompted William Cullen Bryant's famous poem, "Thanatopsis." *Thanatos* is the Greek word for death.

> So live, that when thy summons comes to join
> The innumerable caravan, that moves
> To that mysterious realm, where each shall take
> His chamber in the silent halls of death,
> Thou go not, like the quarry-slave at night,
> Scourged to his dungeon, but, sustained and soothed
> By an unfaltering trust, approach thy grave
> Like one who wraps the drapery of his couch
> About him, and lies down to pleasant dreams.

Despite the comfort in these lovely lines, the Scriptures do not teach that the soul literally sleeps in death.

Luke 16 records a story which some view as a parable, although it appears to be an illustration. In it Jesus taught that the dead reside in Hades where there is a division between the souls of the faithful and the unfaithful. The faithful rest in a place of comfort referred to as "Abraham's bosom," separated by a wide gulf from souls in torment. According to the narrative, the dead see, speak, and feel emotion and also have the powers of memory and recognition.

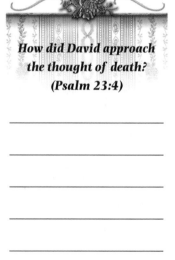

How did David approach the thought of death? (Psalm 23:4)

Hades is the place where Jesus spent three days and nights after His death on the cross, according to Acts 2:27. It is not to be confused with hell, the place of final torment. (The King James Version incorrectly translates the Hebrew *Sheol* and the Greek *Hades* as "hell" more than forty times.)[2] Because Jesus possessed the keys of death and Hades, the gates of Hades could not prevent Him from rising victoriously from the dead (Matthew 16:18; Revelation 1:18). His

---

2. Owen Olbricht, *Beyond Death's Door* (Delight, AR: Gospel Light), 34-35.

resurrection gives hope to all who die in Him; and although Job could not have known these things apart from divine revelation, he felt that he would live to see God (Job 19:26).

God can remove the sting of death.

For those who make preparation, death loses its sting, according to Paul, who found himself looking forward to it in a way that many would find hard to understand (1 Corinthians 15:55; Philippians 1:23).

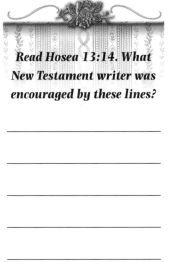

Read Hosea 13:14. What New Testament writer was encouraged by these lines?

_____

_____

_____

_____

_____

J. J. Turner, in his book *Life, Death, and Beyond*, states that "everyone thinks about life and death. All men desire something beyond the grave. Most men, also, have a change of attitude toward death as they stand at its door."[3] Those who face it unprepared are left with the fear and anxiety expressed by the patriot Thomas Paine. "Lord, help me! O God, what have I done to suffer so much? But there is no God! But if there should be, what will become of me hereafter?"[4] Contrast his fear with that of one who has made preparations for the hereafter.

My Aunt Mary died at the age of eighty-five. Perhaps because she grew up as the eldest of nine children during the *Great Depression*, she always seemed to take life's hardships in stride. Legally blind in her latter years, she remained cheerful because she was a faithful Christian who kept her spiritual sight focused on positive things. Near death she took comfort in Philippians 4:8, Paul's list of the things we should think on. She did not want prayers for recovery because she sensed that her transition was near, and she was prepared. She leaned on her faith, and she left this life with dignity.

Live until you die.

One recent publication lists suicide as the eighth leading cause of death in America. It claims that there are twenty non-fatal attempts for each completed suicide.[5] For all of his suffering, Job recognized the fundamental principle stated

---

3. J. J. Turner, *Life, Death, and Beyond* (Florence: Lambert Book House, 1988), 12.
4. Ibid.
5. Bill Flatt, *Building a Healthy Family* (Nashville: Christian Communications, 1993), 200.

in Job 1:21: "The Lord gave, and the Lord has taken away." God is the giver of life, and we are not our own (1 Corinthians 6:19). David said in Psalm 100:3, "It is He who has made us, and not we ourselves; we are His people and the sheep of His pasture."

God has authorized governments to use capital punishment as an instrument of justice (Exodus 21:12; Romans 13:4), but He does not license individuals to take human life. Those who justify abortion on demand on the grounds that a woman controls her own body should note Job's recognition that God made him in the womb (Job 31:15). Unborn children are His.

Read Job 12:10. What was Job's view of human life?

_____

_____

_____

_____

_____

Life is too precious to waste. While in his agony, Job did not envision the many happy years ahead. It is likely that he never knew why he had suffered, but He learned to trust the One who holds the world in the palm of His hand.

Points To Remember

- ◆ God cares for those who grieve.
- ◆ The righteous are at peace in death.
- ◆ God can remove the sting of death.
- ◆ Live until you die.

Points To Ponder

- ◆ *"May you live all the days of your life." Jonathan Swift*
- ◆ *When we die, we leave behind us all we have, and take with us all we are.*
- ◆ *"Death is the golden key which opens the palace of eternity." Milton*
- ◆ *"Is death the last sleep? No, it is the last and final awakening." Walter Scott*

~9~

Can Any Good Thing Come Out of Nazareth?

Beth and Blake Gustin

Some in the assembly marveled at Jesus' gracious speech,
but the majority concluded that He could not have anything profound to say,
because he was just the carpenter, one of their own.

*Jesus said to them, "A prophet is not without honor
except in his hometown."*

Matthew 13:57

109

And Nathanael

said to him, *"Can any good thing come*

out of Nazareth?" Philip said to

him, "Come and see."

John 1:46

Can Any Good Thing Come Out of Nazareth?

A Lesson on Prejudice

John 1:35–51

The Promise Fulfilled: A Mystery Revealed

God's Prophets: Men on Fire

Seventeen books of prophecy comprise the last section of the Old Testament. The first five—Isaiah, Jeremiah, Lamentations, Ezekiel, and Daniel—bear the title of Major Prophets because of their length. The Minor Prophets make up the final twelve books of the Testament.

The prophets were men and a small handful of women—Miriam, Deborah, Anna, for example—who spoke about God or for God.[1] Their messages never originated with themselves, "but men moved by the Holy Spirit spoke from God" according to 2 Peter 1:21. One has summarized their role as that of "men who spoke, under the influence of the Holy Spirit, the words and thoughts of God, whether relating to the past, the present, or the future."[2]

The Hebrew word for prophet means "to boil up like a fountain," which prompted one author to comment that the prophets were men who had something to say and had to say it.[3] Jeremiah typified them well, writing about a burning fire in his bones which he could not contain, even when his outspokenness got him into serious trouble. Many of the prophets spoke out about social injustice and the consequences of it. Some were also able to look into the future and foretell events relating to the coming Messiah.

When Adam and Eve sinned, they brought condemnation and death into the world. In Genesis 3:15 we noted the first important clue as to how God planned to solve this monumental problem—by the coming of a male child, born of woman, who would destroy forever the power of Satan. Jesus described God's magnificent plan as a mystery, telling His disciples: "To you has been given the mystery of the kingdom of God" (Mark 4:11). Paul made reference to this mystery more than a dozen times in his epistles, writing in Romans 16:25–26 that the mystery, kept secret for long ages past, was being made

---

1. Homer Hailey, *A Commentary on the Minor Prophets* (Grand Rapids: Baker Book House, 1972), 15.
2. Ibid., 15-16.
3. Ibid., 65.

known to all nations, resulting in obedient faith. One very important role of the prophets was to provide details as to how and when it would be revealed.

False prophets existed from earliest times, according to Jeremiah 23:32, and Peter warned that false teachers would follow after them (2 Peter 2:1–2). God therefore made the test of a true prophet very simple: anyone claiming to speak for Him whose prophecies failed was false and deserved to die (Deuteronomy 18:20–22). Interest has flourished in recent years in Nostradamus, the sixteenth-century astrologer and physician hailed by some as a great foreteller of the future, even though his predictions were vague and subject to many different interpretations. The Old Testament prophets, on the other hand, left more than three hundred specific prophecies about the Messiah, all of which Jesus of Nazareth fulfilled.

More than seven hundred years before Jesus' birth, Isaiah, often designated the "Messianic Prophet," received God's call and began to prophesy in Jerusalem. He foretold the coming of God's Servant Immanuel, to be born of a virgin (Isaiah 7:14; 42:1). Isaiah saw the appearance of John the Baptist (40:3) and Christ's anointing by the Holy Spirit (61:1). He prophesied that the Son of God would be poor (53:2), compassionate (40:11), and without guile (53:9). He would perform miracles (35:5–6) but would become a stumbling stone to the Jews and a rock of offense to many (8:14). In the last days His teaching would result in salvation for Gentiles as well as Jews (2:1–3).

The Messianic Prophets

Isaiah saw God's Servant suffering persecution unjustly and in silence (Isaiah 53:7), yet making intercession for those who were afflicting Him (53:12). He would be executed as a common criminal but buried with the rich (53:9). The fifty-third chapter alone contains fifteen separate prophecies fulfilled in Jesus and has prompted this observation:

> Unbelievers have searched heaven and earth, the living and the dead, to find anybody but Jesus to fit the chapter's statements; but nobody except Jesus fits. Further, it would be impossible for anybody else purposely to arrange his life so as to make Isaiah 53 tell of Him.[4]

Another writer suggests: "Mathematically, it has been calculated that the probability of any individual fulfilling just eight of the prophecies is staggering."[5] The prophet Daniel first used the word *Messiah* in Daniel 9:25–26.

---

4. Hugo McCord, *Messianic Prophecies* (n.p., n.d.), 44.
5. Peter Stoner, *Science Speaks* (Chicago: Moody Press, 1963), 100-107.

God had visited King Nebuchadnezzar with the vision of a great image representing the future empires of Medo-Persia, Greece, and Rome. He showed Daniel the coming of the kingdom of God during the days of the Roman Empire (Daniel 2:44), even pinpointing the very year of the Messiah's birth hundreds of years in the future (9:25).

Malachi, the last prophetic voice of the Old Testament, revealed that Messiah's coming would be announced by a messenger reminiscent of the prophet Elijah (Malachi 4:5). And then there followed four hundred years of silence from God, a period in which anticipation was building in the hearts of people waiting for the promise to be fulfilled.

The Turning Point of History

Every great mystery has its turning point shortly before the ending is revealed. After the death of the last Old Testament prophet, a number of events began to come together. The Persian Empire collapsed, and Alexander the Great unified the ancient world by spreading the Greek culture and language everywhere. He commissioned a group of scholars to translate the law of Moses into Greek, with the result that the whole world had access to the mystery God was about to reveal. The Jews, meanwhile, were experiencing a renewed interest in their own heritage, and Jewish boys were learning to read Hebrew in synagogue schools using the Scriptures for a text. Truly, God was at work preparing the world for the greatest event in all of history. And then "when the fulness of the time came, God sent forth His Son, born of a woman . . . that we might receive the adoption as sons" (Galatians 4:4–5).

Luke records that in the days of Herod, God's angel appeared to an Israelite priest named Zacharias and informed him that he and his wife Elizabeth were going to have a son, a child filled with the Holy Spirit from his mother's womb. His mission was to go forth in the spirit of Elijah to make ready a people prepared for the Lord (Luke 1:17). It was a clear fulfillment of Malachi's prophecy.

Six months later the angel Gabriel appeared to a young virgin in the city of Nazareth with these words:

> Do not be afraid, Mary; for you have found favor with God. And behold, you will conceive in your womb, and bear a son, and you shall name Him Jesus. He will be great, and will be called the Son of the Most High; and the Lord God will give Him the throne of His father David; and He will reign over the house of Jacob forever; and His kingdom will have no end (Luke 1:30–33).

The angel also appeared to Joseph, her husband-to-be, instructing him that the child conceived in Mary was of the Holy Spirit. They should name him Jesus 'Jehovah is Salvation' because, said Gabriel, "It is He who will save His people from their sins" (Matthew 1:20–21).

"In the Fullness of Time" (Galatians 4:4)

Joseph obeyed the angel and married his betrothed but "kept her a virgin until she gave birth to a Son" (Matthew 1:25). It was during the days of her pregnancy that Caesar Augustus issued a decree that all of the Roman world should be taxed. It forced each family to enroll in their ancestral home, so Mary and Joseph made an eighty-mile journey from Nazareth to Bethlehem of Judea since both were of the lineage of David.

Because they could find no space in the inn, they had to take lodging among the livestock. Tradition claims their shelter may have been a cave outside Bethlehem. There Mary gave birth to her Son, whom they named Jesus, and laid Him in a manger.

There is no indication as to the month of Jesus' birth, other than Luke's account that shepherds were watching their flocks in nearby fields. Because winters in Judea are wet and chilly, some have suggested the time was during the spring lambing season, when shepherds would be in the fields tending their ewes. It was not until three hundred years later that men designated December 25 as a religious holiday in order to coincide with a traditional Roman festival celebrated on that date.[6]

The Savior's birth was heralded by an angel who spoke to the wondering shepherds, saying, "Fear not, for, behold, I bring you good tidings of great joy, which shall be to all people. For unto you is born this day in the city of David a Savior, which is Christ the Lord" (Luke 2:10–11 KJV). When they went into Bethlehem, they found the babe just as the angel had said.

"God with Us" (Matthew 1:23)

Other people recognized His divinity in the weeks that followed. Mary and Joseph took the child at forty days into Jerusalem where they presented him in the temple as the law required. They offered a gift of two doves or two pigeons, which sufficed for those too poor to afford a lamb (Leviticus 12:1–8; Luke 2:24). A devout man named Simeon spotted them, and taking the babe in his arms he

---

6. J. J. Packer, Merrill Tenney, and William White, *The Bible Almanac* (Nashville: Thomas Nelson, 1980), 515.

said, "Now, Lord, let Thy bondservant depart in peace . . . for my eyes have seen Thy salvation . . . a light of revelation to the Gentiles and the glory of Thy people Israel" (Luke 2:29–32). He recognized that this child fulfilled Isaiah's vision of a great light shining among the Gentiles (Isaiah 60:1–3). The elderly prophetess Anna likewise gave thanks when she saw the young Jesus and spoke of Him to all who would listen.

At some point—perhaps weeks or months later—magi specializing in astrology, medicine, and science arrived from the East, following an unusual star. They came laden with expensive gifts and must have caused quite a stir, for when Herod heard of it, it troubled him as well as all Jerusalem. It was through the prophecy in Micah 5:2 that Herod was able to ascertain where they might find the child. But God warned Joseph in a dream to take his family into Egypt, for the king would seek to destroy Him. Joseph arose by night and obeyed the Lord's command.

At God's direction the magi did not report the young child's whereabouts as Herod had directed. The infuriated king then issued a cruel edict for the slaughter of all male children in Bethlehem, two years and under (cf. Jeremiah 31:15). Mercifully this king, who was not above killing some of his own wives and children, died shortly thereafter; and God summoned Joseph home, fulfilling Hosea 11:1, "Out of Egypt have I called my son." Herod's son Archelaus was then ruling in Judea, so God directed Joseph back to Nazareth of Galilee, where the lad Jesus grew into manhood.

The Lamb of God

Jewish fathers began educating their children at the age of three, teaching their sons to recite portions of Scripture such as Deuteronomy 6:4–9.[7] The law, or Torah 'instruction', was the basis of their education; and much of the training was oral, consisting of questions and answers about the stories of God's dealings with His people. The sacred feasts also provided parents with an opportunity to explain their traditions. There is no biblical evidence that Jesus had any miraculous ability as a child, but He must have possessed a keen, inquisitive mind. We can only imagine His fascination with the Passover observance, for example, and the growing realization as He matured that He was to become that paschal lamb.

---

7. Elrose Hunter and Paul Marsh, *Bible Encyclopedia for the Family* (Nashville, Thomas Nelson, 1982), 245-253.

Joseph and Mary's family grew to include four more sons and at least two daughters (Matthew 13:55–56). Theirs must have been a busy household, with the boys likely learning the carpentry trade from Joseph, and their daughters learning from Mary how to become capable wives and mothers. As the oldest child, Jesus learned responsibility and compassion at home while mastering the basics of reading and writing in the synagogue school for boys. Using the Aramaic language, He would have memorized large portions of Scripture and participated in arguing the finer points of the law with His rabbi (teacher).

He must have been a master pupil. Luke records that His parents, like all faithful Jews, went to the Passover every year. "And when he became twelve, they went up [there] according to the custom of the Feast" (Luke 2:42). Most twelve-year-old boys might have viewed the trip as a great adventure, but Jesus was drawn to seek out the doctors of the law to observe their debate. So intent was His concentration that His parents located Him three days later "sitting in the midst of the teachers, both listening to them, and asking them questions" (Luke 2:46). When Mary chastened Him for causing them some anxiety, Jesus seemed surprised that they had not known where to find Him. He answered her, "Why is it that you were looking for Me? Did you not know that I had to be in My Father's house?" (Luke 2:49). What a lot Mary had to think about in those early years! (Luke 2:19, 51).

Luke records that it was in the fifteenth year of Tiberius Caesar, when Pontius Pilate was governor of Judea, that the word of God came to John, the promised son of Zacharias, and he began to preach the baptism of repentance for the forgiveness of sins. Many people wondered if he might be the Christ of prophecy, whose time they knew was near (Luke 3:15); but John assured them, "I am not the Christ." Quoting Isaiah, John told them, "I am a voice of one crying in the wilderness, 'Make straight the way of the Lord'" (John 1:20–23).

So it was that Jesus, being about thirty years old, came to the Jordan River near Bethany where John was baptizing and requested that John immerse Him. In some of the most beautiful language in all the Bible, John announced:

> Behold, the Lamb of God who takes away the sin of the world! This is He on behalf of whom I said, "After me comes a Man who has a higher rank than I, for He existed before me." And I did not recognize Him, but in order that He might be manifested to Israel, I came baptizing in water (John 1:29–31).

As He came up out of the water, the Spirit of God descended upon Jesus in the form of a dove and God spoke from Heaven, announcing, "This is My beloved Son, in whom I am well pleased" (Matthew 3:17).

"We Have Found Him!"

Two of John's followers, Andrew and Peter, were convinced that Jesus was the Christ, the Messiah, and they quickly shared the news with Philip, one from their hometown of Bethsaida. Philip, in turn, hurried to his friend Nathanael with the message: "We have found Him of whom Moses in the Law and also the Prophets wrote, Jesus of Nazareth, the son of Joseph" (John 1:45). Nathanael must have listened with interest, but he wondered aloud, "Can any good thing come out of Nazareth?" Still, at Philip's insistence he was willing to investigate. How easily a closed mind could have prevented him from getting to know the Savior of the world!

John writes: "Jesus saw Nathanael coming to him" (John 1:47). Jesus saw a man in whom there was no slyness or cunning—and He paid him a rare compliment. When Nathanael asked, "How do you know me?" Jesus replied, "Before Philip called you, when you were under the fig tree, I saw you." Whatever Jesus had observed, it caused Nathanael to quickly abandon all prejudice. "Rabbi," he said, "You are the Son of God; You are the King of Israel." He became one of a growing group of disciples who left all to follow Jesus.

Am I guilty of prejudice?

The word *prejudice* comes from the Latin *prae* 'before' and *judicium* 'judgment'. It is "an opinion held in disregard of facts that contradict it; bias." How easily we succumb to prejudice! I recall a sociology professor who introduced a discussion of prejudice by charging that we were all guilty of it, then going on to make his case to a classroom of skeptics. The respected journalist Edward R. Murrow once commented: "Everyone is a prisoner of his own experiences. No one can eliminate prejudices—just recognize them." Recognizing prejudice will require us to understand what it is *not*.

God expects me to make judgments.

Taking a moral stand does not prove prejudice. A common criticism leveled against Christians who take a biblical but politically incorrect position on moral issues is that they are guilty of judging. Have you ever noticed that the Lord's command in Matthew 7:1 that we "judge not" is one of the few verses of Scripture some people can quote? Another is John 8:11, where Jesus declared to the woman taken in adultery, "Neither do I condemn you." In His admonition, "From now on sin no more," the Lord made plain, however, that her conduct had been wrong. The Bible does not forbid making judgments of right and wrong. If it did, how could anyone ever heed the warning to "examine everything carefully; hold fast to that which is good; abstain from every form of evil"?

Why is Matthew 7:1 such an oft-quoted verse?

(1 Thessalonians 5:21–22). It does forbid a double standard of hypocrisy which sees faults in others that we excuse in ourselves.

Jesus frequently judged some things to be wrong. He accused the moneychangers in the temple of turning that sacred house of prayer into a den of robbers (Luke 19:46). In Matthew 23 He brought a blistering condemnation against the conduct of the Pharisees in language that many today would consider intolerant. Paul also wrote to the Corinthian church concerning a case of immorality: "I . . . have already judged him who has so committed this" (1 Corinthians 5:3). He also reminded the church of their obligation to settle disputes among themselves, adding, "Or do you not know that the saints will judge the world?" (1 Corinthians 6:2).

Tolerance, however, is becoming the theme of our day. Opinion polls suggest that our nation is becoming more accepting of lax moral standards. "Thou shalt not judge" has been called America's *Eleventh Commandment* by sociologist Alan Wolfe.[8] In his book *The Death of Outrage*, William Bennett adds that those who celebrate America's growing tolerance should consider that "the defining mark of a good republic is . . . the willingness of its citizens to make judgments about things that matter."[9]

Prejudice is akin to blindness.

Soon after Jesus began His ministry, He returned to His hometown of Nazareth and entered the synagogue on a Sabbath day, as He had done count-

---

8. William Bennett, *The Death of Outrage* (New York: The Free Press, 1998), 120.
9. Ibid., 121.

less times before (Luke 4:16). When He stood to read, He selected a passage from Isaiah:

> The spirit of the Lord is upon Me, because He anointed Me to preach the gospel to the poor. He has sent Me to proclaim release to the captives, and recovery of sight to the blind, to set free those who are downtrodden, to proclaim the favorable year of the Lord (Luke 4:18).

Isaiah condemned the spiritual blindness of his day, saying, "Look, you blind, that you may see . . . You have seen many things, but you do not observe them" (Isaiah 42:18–20). Jesus' choice of this passage and His allusion to the proverb that "no prophet is welcome in his home town" was an obvious suggestion that they were prejudiced. Some in the assembly marveled at His gracious speech, but the majority concluded that He could not have anything profound to say because He was just "the carpenter," one of their own. They cast Him out of their city, and from then on Jesus took up residence in Capernaum, with no mention being made of His returning to Nazareth again.

Prejudice thrives in darkness.

According to Genesis 1:2, the world was originally filled with darkness until Jehovah said, "Let there be light." Everything God made was good, but sin began to envelope the world in a spiritual blackness. God was visible in nature (Romans 1:20), and the Law and the Prophets become a foot lamp to give guidance, however dim (Psalm 119:105).

Karl's grandfather, Papa Craun, told of walking through the hollow—a small valley abounding in plant and animal life—many nights with nothing but a lantern.

The light was weak, but he was thankful for it! That small light, vital as it was, typifies the Old Law. It served its purpose well until Jesus, the Morning Star, arose and dispelled the night (2 Peter 1:19). Thus, Jesus could say, "I am the light of the world; he who follows Me shall not walk in the darkness, but shall have the light of life" (John 8:12).

Even though light has come into the world, spiritual blindness keeps some people from seeing it. Nature itself teaches that prolonged exposure to darkness produces temporary blindness, a fact that we experience whenever we go from a darkened room into the brilliance of sunlight. The gospel has the power to open eyes that have been blind, according to Acts 26:18. Yet Jesus knew that many people would choose to remain in the dark (John 3:19–21). As one has

observed, "The mind of a bigot is like the pupil of the eye; the more light you pour upon it, the more it will contract."

Prejudice alienates me from others.

The world is full of prejudices; if we are honest we can recognize them in ourselves more often than we would like to admit. It is sometimes easier to hold onto them than to consider new ways of thinking. Young people often view the older generation as "stuck in their ways"; the mature, in turn, can be overly critical of the young. Different income levels tend to cause snobbishness and distrust, even among brethren (James 2:1–4). Prejudices arise between the educated and uneducated, between people of different racial or religious backgrounds, and among males and females. Quite often we must deal with preconceived notions that many outside the church entertain toward those of us within. Whenever we become the brunt of someone else's prejudice, we should resolve more than ever to rid ourselves of it. Paul reminded the Galatian churches, composed of Jews as well as Gentiles, that we are "all one in Christ Jesus" (Galatians 3:28). The world should be able to recognize us by our love for each other rather than our distrust (John 13:35).

Points To Remember

- God expects me to make judgments.
- Prejudice is akin to blindness.
- Prejudice thrives in darkness.
- Prejudice alienates me from others.

Points To Ponder

- *"A number of people think they are thinking when they are merely rearranging their prejudices."* William James
- *"Beware prejudices. They are like rats, and men's minds are like traps; prejudices get in easily, but it is doubtful if they ever get out."* Francis Jeffrey
- *Prejudice is being down on something you're not up on.*
- *You're prejudiced when you weigh the facts with your thumb on the scale.*

10

Why Are You So Fearful?

Janie and "Cuzin" Rick Hewgley

If you can't be content with what you have received,
be thankful for what you have escaped.

*"With thanksgiving let your requests be made known to God.
And the peace of God, which surpasses all comprehension,
shall guard your hearts and your minds in Christ Jesus."*

Philippians 4:6-7

And he said

to them, "Why are you

so fearful? How is it that

you have no faith?"

Mark 4:40 KJV

Why Are You So Fearful?
A Lesson on Anxiety

Mark 4:35–41

Jesus: Son of God and Son of Man

The Historical Jesus

Most scholars believe the birth of Jesus of Nazareth occurred in the year 4 B.C. It was popular at one time for skeptics to question whether He ever really lived, although very few dare to suggest it anymore. Even they have found the historical evidence for His existence overwhelming, confirmed by believers and non-believers alike. Claudius Tacitus, the greatest of the Roman historians, mentions Him, as well as the Jewish historian Josephus. In fact, altogether there are over a dozen ancient non-Christian documents attesting to His life. Considering that there exist over five thousand New Testament manuscripts, or parts of manuscripts, which provide details about His life, the evidence is undeniable![1]

Most historians place the date of Jesus' crucifixion in A.D. 30 and conclude that His life spanned slightly more than thirty-three years. He lived it out in an area roughly equivalent to that of Massachusetts and Connecticut combined. During those years He never earned a degree, wrote a book, or ran for public office. He never owned any real estate or accumulated any measurable wealth. Yet He has left a mark on history which is unparalleled.

The Skeptic's Jesus

In the last century skeptics who were unable to disprove the existence of Jesus turned their attention, instead, to challenging His authenticity. Efforts like the *Jesus Seminar* have tried to discredit the miraculous elements in the Gospels. One television documentary has claimed that Jesus misunderstood His mission and never expected to be arrested and crucified. *Newsweek* magazine published an article entitled "Why Did He Die?" claiming that it was because He "challenged established sacred teaching on His own authority as a self-designated spokesman for God."[2] In other words, He brought about His own demise due to His political miscalculations. All of these views are foreign to the gospel, which

---

1. Gary Habermas, *The Historical Jesus* (Joplin, MO: The College Press, 1996), 27.
2. "Why Did He Die?" *Newsweek*, April 24, 2000.

reveals that Jesus' death was purposed before the foundation of the world. Only His precious blood could redeem sinful mankind from the penalty of death.

Jesus of the Gospels

The first four New Testament books have been designated *Gospels,* although there is but one gospel message. Matthew, Mark, and Luke, the Synoptic Gospels, differ slightly from John's account. Matthew wrote for the Jews, while Mark addressed the Romans; and Luke, the Greeks. John's unique record is for Christians in general. All four accounts of the life of Jesus were completed during the first century by eyewitnesses or persons very close to a witness. (Matthew and John were apostles, Mark was a companion to Peter, and Luke was closely associated with Paul.) Mark's introduction states what each of the others also convey, that Jesus Christ is the Son of God (Mark 1:1).

The world could not grasp the idea of the Creator's coming in the flesh. John wrote concerning Jesus that "He was in the world, and the world was made through Him, and the world did not know Him" (John 1:10). The Jews were expecting a political savior to return their nation to its glory days. A humble carpenter from Nazareth who taught self-sacrifice hardly fit their image of the Messiah.

Jesus studied the prophecies from His youth and at some point became aware of who He was. He understood the price He would pay, and the human side of His nature dreaded the thought of it. He knew exactly what the prophets had foretold—that He would be rejected by His own, hated without reason, betrayed by a friend, spat upon and abused, crucified like a common criminal, and forsaken for a time by God Himself. He chose to fulfill His role, saying,

> I am the good shepherd; and I know My own, and My own know Me, even as the Father knows Me and I know the Father; and I lay down My life for the sheep . . . No one has taken it away from Me, but I lay it down on My own initiative. I have authority to lay it down, and I have authority to take it up again. This commandment I received from My Father (John 10:14–18).

The Ministering Jesus

After Jesus was baptized, He began a ministry of about three years confined mostly to the region of Galilee. It was at a wedding in Cana that He performed His first miracle, turning water into wine. The signs continued when He went up to Jerusalem for the Passover, causing many people to believe in Him. He was drawing quite a following, including men like Nicodemus, a ruler among the

Jews. On the way home some of the Samaritans also believed, after He spent two days teaching in their village of Sychar. Back in Galilee those who had seen Him working miracles in Jerusalem started to spread His fame throughout the region, and it grew as He spoke in many of their synagogues (Luke 4:14–15; John 4:45).

During this early phase the crowds were enthusiastic, but there were times of discouragement for Jesus as well. Herod arrested John the Baptist, which could only be viewed as ominous for Jesus and His followers. And it must have been very disappointing when the people of His own hometown rejected Him.

One Sabbath day in Capernaum He healed a demon-possessed man in the synagogue, and by evening crowds were bringing other demoniacs to Him. Some of the exorcised demons were crying out, "You are the Son of God!" until Jesus forbade them from prematurely making that confession.

On another day in the same city He healed a paralytic. When Jesus said to the man, "Friend, your sins are forgiven you" it created no small dissension (Luke 5:20). While some were glorifying God at His saying, others in the crowd were amazed and even fearful. All of this was fuel for the scribes and Pharisees who were silently collecting evidence of blasphemy against Jesus.

During this time Jesus was grooming a band of disciples whom He would send out as apostles. With the calling of Matthew, a publican or tax-collector, the scribes and Pharisees began a campaign of public criticism, complaining that Jesus was socializing with sinners. They noted that He was healing people on the Sabbath day and disregarding some of their traditions. His answer was that the Sabbath was made for man, but when He added that the Son of Man was Lord even of the Sabbath, it infuriated them (Mark 2:27–28). Because they could not answer His logic that it is more lawful to do good on the Sabbath than to do harm (Luke 6:9), they were filled with rage and took counsel with the Herodians as to how they could destroy Him (Mark 3:6).

The pressures upon Jesus must have been intense, and He often spent long hours in prayer. Luke records how He went upon the mountain to pray before appointing the twelve. Scholars tell us the setting may have been the Horns of Hattin, a twin-peaked elevation overlooking the Sea of Galilee, which had a magnificent view.[3] In that beautiful and serene setting, He communed with the Father and found strength to plan the final months of His ministry. The next morning Jesus descended with them to a level plain, possibly the plain of

---

3. Charles Pfeiffer, *Baker's Bible Atlas* (Grand Rapids: Baker Book House, 1973), 204.

Gennesaret, where He sat down with the disciples and began an intensive session of teaching which we call the *Sermon on the Mount.*

The Master Teacher

From simple, ordinary objects He drew powerful, memorable lessons with eternal truths. He was about to send His disciples out with nothing but their faith, so He challenged them to trust in God's providential care. "Look at the birds of the air," He said, "that they do not sow, neither do they reap, nor gather into barns, and yet your heavenly Father feeds them. Are you not worth much more than they?" (Matthew 6:26). Concerning the wildflowers He reminded them, "If God so arrays the grass of the field . . . will He not much more do so for you, O men of little faith?" (Matthew 6:30). They would recall those promises on an occasion that later arose.

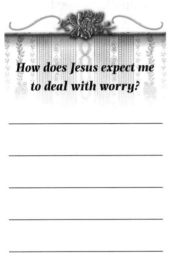

How does Jesus expect me to deal with worry?

There came a day when Jesus had been teaching the multitudes from a boat, because the press of the crowds was so great. In the evening, He left the multitude and headed across the lake, being so wearied that He immediately retired to the rear of the boat and fell asleep. One of the sudden squalls which are so common on the Sea of Galilee arose, and the boat began to be battered about and filled with water. The disciples were frightened and awoke Jesus, crying out, "Master, Master, we are perishing!" (Luke 8:24). Rousing from His sleep, He rebuked the winds and the sea, and there was immediate calm. "Why are ye so fearful? how is it that you have no faith?" He asked them (Mark 4:40 KJV). Their reaction helps us to see that their faith still needed time to grow. "Who . . . is this," they wondered, "that He commands even the winds and the water, and they obey Him?" (Luke 8:25).

Can I really win over worry?

The writer of Hebrews reminds us that Jesus is able to sympathize with all our weaknesses because He has experienced the same struggles that we go through (Hebrews 4:15). That being the case, if anyone ever had to deal with stress and anxiety, surely He did. How, we wonder, was Jesus able to face each day with the realization that He was destined for rejection and an agonizing death? How could He say to the disciples, "Take no thought for your life"? (Matthew 6:25 KJV). Wuest, in his *Word Studies in the Greek New Testament*, states that the Greek literally means, "Stop perpetually worrying."[4]

If it is possible, then, to overcome worry, how do we go about it? It seems that stress is a constant factor in life. Jesus certainly had concerns, and He attracted great throngs of people needing help with their problems. Even during the agony of His crucifixion, His mother's welfare was on His mind (John 19:26–27). Paul was concerned daily for the churches He had established (2 Corinthians 11:28). Both men were able to practice what Peter advised in 1 Peter 5:7—that we cast our anxieties upon God, who cares for us. We do that by making some very specific choices.

Why does everyone need a foundation in life?

Build a foundation of faith.

Jesus taught that everyone will experience some storms in his life. He illustrated that point with the story of a wise man who built his house upon a rock. "And the rain descended, and the floods came, and the winds blew, and burst against that house: and yet it did not fall, because it had been founded upon the rock" (Matthew 7:24–25). Laying a firm foundation of faith makes all the difference in whether we survive or collapse when life's storms do hit. That is why Jesus told the disciples that they must "seek first His kingdom and His righteousness" (Matthew 6:33). God promises in return to

4. Kenneth S. Wuest, *Word Studies in the Greek New Testament* (Grand Rapids: Eerdmans, 1973), 43.

provide the things which we need. David, whose life was threatened on numerous occasions, had learned that lesson, writing in Psalm 55:22 that the Lord sustains those who cast their burdens upon Him. We lay the foundation of faith by giving God His rightful place in our lives.

Be willing to attack your fears.

Psychologists tell us that fear is the underlying cause of anxiety. In the 1960s, Dr. S. I. McMillan produced his best-selling book, *None of These Diseases*, in which he claimed that fear is responsible for a wide range of illnesses.[5] He went on to report that research now seems to blame most disease on mental stress, rather than on bacteria.[6]

What causes you the most anxiety? Is fear a factor?

Fear does not come from God. He wants us to possess power and love and discipline, according to 2 Timothy 1:7. In the Scriptures fear often results from guilt, as in the case of Adam and Eve who hid from God because they had disobeyed (Genesis 3:10). David found that unconfessed sin caused his body to waste away, and it was only when he acknowledged it to God that his peace of mind returned (Psalm 32:3–5). Our confidence grows as our love for God matures (1 John 4:16–18). A case in point is the virtuous woman of Proverbs 31 who was not afraid of the snow for her household because she had made provisions for them. She worked hard (v. 13), planned ahead (v. 16), practiced benevolence (v. 20), and trusted God (v. 30), with the result that she was able to smile at the future (v. 25).

A popular book, *The Tough-Minded Optimist*, contains a chapter entitled "Never Be Afraid of Anybody or Anything." The author stresses that one must overcome the fear of failure if he is to enjoy success in his undertakings. God demonstrated this to Gideon, when he had him rid his army of all those who were fearful (Judges 7:2–7). The story illustrates that God wanted cautious men who were willing to act on faith. We must examine our fears if we would control anxiety.

---

5. McMillan, *None of These Diseases* (Old Tappen, NJ: Revell Co., 1980), 82.
6. Ibid., 22.

Adopt a Positive Attitude.

Psychologist William James wrote that human beings can change the outer aspects of their lives by changing the inner attitudes of their minds. The truth of his statement is illustrated in the life of the apostle Paul. Despite the many adversities he suffered, Paul kept from being overwhelmed by drawing on a higher strength. "I can do all things through Him who strengthens me," he wrote in Philippians 4:13.

Attitudes are immensely important. They are the filters through which we view everything in our sight.[7] The good news is that we can program our attitudes to be positive, even when things around us are negative. Paul's joy remained boundless in spite of hardships (2 Corinthians 7:4). Clad in chains, he wrote the church at Philippi urging them to "rejoice in the Lord always" (Philippians 4:4). Paul just refused to give in to a spirit of pessimism.

Some scholars have concluded that Jesus was a man given to melancholy because Isaiah portrays Him as "a man of sorrows, acquainted with grief" (Isaiah 53:3). One even claimed that "he was never seen to laugh." That seems highly unlikely, given the humor that is evident in many of His parables and illustrations. It is possible to laugh even in distressing situations; one writer has noted that "far from laughter being incompatible with anguish, it is often the natural expression of deep pain."[8]

Elton Trueblood, in *The Humor of Christ*, has commented that humor is a characteristic of the Christian, not because he is blind to injustice and suffering, but because he is convinced that these, in the light of the divine sovereignty, are never ultimate. Though he can be sad, and is often perplexed, he is never really worried. The well-known humor of the Christian is not a way of denying the tears, but rather a way of affirming something which is deeper than tears.[9] Attitude makes all the difference in how well we weather life's storms.

How did Jesus maintain a positive attitude?

---

7. Shad Helmstetter, *What To Say When You Talk to Yourself* (New York: Pocket Books, 1982), 163.
8. Elton Trueblood, *The Humor of Christ* (New York: Harper and Row, 1964), 23.
9. Ibid., 32.

You Mustn't Quit

When things go wrong, as they sometimes will,
When the road you're trudging seems all uphill,
When the funds are low and the debts are high
And you want to smile, but you have to sigh,
When care is pressing you down a bit,
Rest if you must—but never quit.

Cultivate gratitude for what you have.

There is a strong connection between gratitude and peace of mind, according to Colossians 3:15. Paul said it this way: "With thanksgiving let your requests be made known to God. And the peace of God, which surpasses all comprehension, shall guard your hearts and your minds in Christ Jesus" (Philippians 4:6–7). Someone has quipped, "If you can't be content with what you have received, be thankful for what you have escaped."

Begin a list of things in your life for which you are grateful. How does it affect your state of mind?

_____

_____

_____

_____

In Charles Dickens' classic, *A Christmas Carol,* Ebenezer Scrooge was a miserable, bitter human being who had no room in his heart for gratitude. But given the opportunity to see his sad, pitiful condition and the tragic end that awaited him, Scrooge begged for and received a second chance. His appreciation was so profound that he became a new man, with an enthusiasm for living that was almost boundless. Someone has wisely observed that the one who forgets the language of gratitude will never be on speaking terms with contentment.

Points To Remember

- ◆ Build a foundation of faith.
- ◆ Be willing to attack your fears.
- ◆ Adopt a positive attitude.
- ◆ Cultivate gratitude for what you have.

Points To Ponder

- ◆ *"Anxiety is a thin stream of fear trickling through the mind. If encouraged, it cuts a channel into which all other thoughts are drained." Arthur Somers Roche*
- ◆ *Anxiety is the interest paid on trouble before it is due.*
- ◆ *When you become wrinkled with care and worry, it's time to have your faith lifted.*
- ◆ *Don't worry too much about what lies ahead. Go as far as you can see, and when you get there, you can see farther.*

11

For What Is a Man Profited?

(center) Great-grandmother, Eliza Wade Hardeman
Children (l to r) John, Willie Pearl, Ella, Evie, and Lon

We must relinquish all claim upon our possessions as being our own, realizing that they, along with our very lives, belong to God.

"Do not work for the food which perishes,
but for the food which endures to eternal life,
which the Son of Man shall give to you."

John 6:27

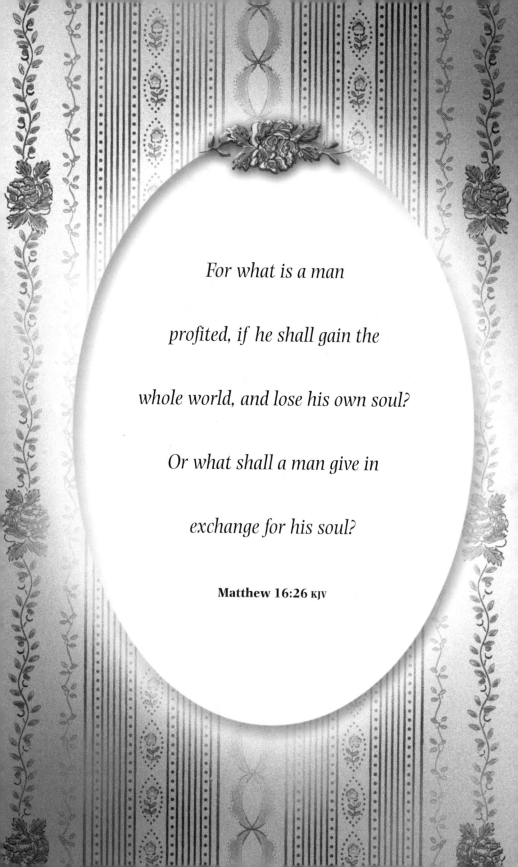

For what is a man

profited, if he shall gain the

whole world, and lose his own soul?

Or what shall a man give in

exchange for his soul?

Matthew 16:26 KJV

For What Is a Man Profited?

A Lesson on Discipleship

Matthew 16:13-28

Preaching the Kingdom

The Message: Spoken in Parables

As Jesus went about His ministry of healing the sick, casting out demons, and raising the dead, He attracted great throngs of people to Him. These signs, as the Bible calls them, served the purpose of confirming His teaching. The message was always the focal point of His ministry; and He often delivered it in parables, which some have called "earthly stories with heavenly meanings."

It prompted the disciples to ask Him why He always used these illustrations, which were sometimes hard to understand. He replied, "To you it has been granted to know the mysteries of the kingdom of heaven, but to them it has not been granted" (Matthew 13:11). The parables allowed honest seekers to understand spiritual truths easily, even if He sometimes had to explain them. Those who constantly sought to trap Him, however, could find very little incriminating in such simple, entertaining stories.

Jesus was also fulfilling Old Testament prophecy. Matthew quotes Psalm 78:2: "I will open my mouth in parables; I will utter things hidden since the foundation of the world" (Matthew 13:35). In private Jesus explained the lessons to the twelve (Mark 4:34), but they were sometimes slow to understand them.

The Mission: Carried Out By Men

The apostles Jesus chose were a diverse group. There were the brothers, Peter and Andrew who were fishermen, and their close friends and partners, James and John, sons of Zebedee. These four were joined by Philip, from their hometown of Bethsaida, and Bartholomew, whom tradition has identified as Nathanael. They included Thomas, called Didymus or "the twin," and Matthew, also named Levi, who made his living as a tax-collector. Completing the group were James the son of Alpheus, Thaddeus, Simon the Zealot, and Judas Iscariot.

Judas kept their money box, from which he pilfered (John 12:6). Jesus must have realized early on that Judas had a weakness for money, for John tells that He knew from the beginning who would betray Him (John 6:64). Still, Jesus entrusted him with the purse and allowed him the freedom to deal treacherously.

As He sent them out to teach, Jesus warned the twelve about the personal risks involved in following Him. "Behold," He said, "I send you out as sheep in the midst of wolves; therefore be shrewd as serpents, and innocent as doves" (Matthew 10:16). The cost of discipleship, He cautioned, would be dear. They would be subject to acts of hatred and persecution from others for His name's sake.

The warning was not lost on them as news came of John the Baptist's execution by Herod. Together, they left by boat for Bethsaida for some private time. This is likely Bethsaida Julias, a wide plain used for grazing on the east bank of the Jordan, the other side of the Sea of Galilee (John 6:1). Although the Scripture doesn't say so, it seems likely that Jesus had John on His mind. These two men were related by birth but very different outwardly (Luke 7:33–34). John lived a secluded life, while Jesus socialized with the common people. But Jesus had the highest regard for John, saying that among those born of women no greater had arisen (Matthew 11:11). He was a man whose entire life was spent preparing for a mission of under three years, and John never forgot that his role was that of best man to the Bridegroom (John 3:29). There was little time, however, to mourn for him.

The Promise: The Bread of Life

The crowds had anticipated His destination, and they ran on ahead (Mark 6:33). Although Jesus had sought privacy, He welcomed the people, according to Luke 9:11. John adds that this great multitude had come to see the signs which Jesus performed on the sick (John 6:2). So He taught and healed until the day was spent. And what followed that evening was a miracle so amazing that all the Gospel writers recorded it.

Mark relates that Jesus felt compassion for the crowd because they were like sheep without a shepherd. Taking a boy's lunch of five barley loaves and two fish, He fed a multitude of five thousand men plus women and children. After everyone had eaten, the apostles collected twelve baskets of left-overs. Already Jesus had demonstrated His mastery over time, space, and infirmity; and now He evidenced His ability to multiply matter itself! The crowd responded by testifying, "This is of a truth the Prophet who is to come into the world" (John 6:14). They were on the verge of taking Him by force and declaring Him their king, when He withdrew from them into the mountain.

That evening the disciples returned to Capernaum by boat, leaving Jesus behind to pray (John 6:17). Mark records more precisely that they were headed back to the fishing village, also known as Bethsaida, home to Peter, Andrew, and Philip (Mark 6:45; John 1:44). The next morning the townspeople could not understand how He had arrived, not knowing, as Matthew, Mark, and John record, that during the night He had walked on the sea to the disciples' boat. They failed to recognize the power demonstrated in the miracle of the loaves and fishes, and it prompted Jesus to note that they were less interested in signs that testified to His divinity than in the bread which He provided (John 6:26).

He cautioned them, "Do not work for the food which perishes, but for the food which endures to eternal life, which the Son of Man shall give to you, for on Him the Father, even God, has set His seal" (John 6:27). Incredibly, some in the crowd asked for another sign so they might believe on Him. They even suggested that Moses proved he was a prophet by providing manna from heaven—hint! hint! Jesus had no intention of bribing them with bread, and He told them so plainly. "I am the bread of life," He said. At this they began to question, "Is not this Jesus, the son of Joseph, whose father and mother we know? How does He now say, 'I have come down out of heaven'?" Jesus began to explain to them that He must die and that His followers must partake of His flesh and blood, but the saying was too hard. Many of them withdrew and did not walk with Him anymore.

From then on Jesus spoke plainly to the apostles about His death in Jerusalem and His resurrection on the third day. Peter took Him aside and chided Him somewhat, saying, "God forbid it, Lord! This shall never happen to You." But Jesus replied, "Get behind Me, Satan! You are a stumbling block to Me; for you are not setting your mind on God's interests, but man's (Matthew 16:23). He went on to assure them that He was ready to suffer and that they must prepare to make their own commitment, saying:

> If anyone wishes to come after Me, let him deny himself, and take up his cross, and follow Me. For whoever wishes to save his life shall lose it; but whoever loses his life for My sake and the gospel's shall save it. For what does it profit a man to gain the whole world, and forfeit his soul? For what shall a man give in exchange for his soul? For whoever is ashamed of Me and My words in this adulterous and sinful generation, the Son of Man will also be ashamed of him when he comes in the glory of His Father with the holy angels (Mark 8:34–38).

In the weeks that followed, their faith would be sorely tested as each man weighed the cost of following Jesus.

Must I pay a price today to serve Jesus?

God's gift is unmerited.

As we noted earlier, the sin of Adam and Eve brought death into the world. The sending of a Savior was God's plan for overcoming the terrible consequence of it (Romans 6:23). Paul explained: "Therefore, just as through one man sin entered into the world, and death through sin and so death spread to all men, because all sinned" (5:12). Adam was a type of Christ, according to Paul's comparison in Romans 5:12–21:

ADAM	CHRIST
◆ brought sin into the world	◆ brought righteousness into the world
◆ brought condemnation	◆ brought justification
◆ brought death to the world	◆ brought life to many

Jesus illustrated the Father's grace in what parable?

The kingdom of heaven may be compared to a certain king who wished to settle accounts with his slaves. And when he had begun to settle them, there was brought to him one who owed him ten thousand talents. But since he did not have the means to repay, his lord commanded him to be sold, along with his wife and children and all that he had, and repayment to be made. The slave therefore falling down, prostrated himself before him, saying, "Have patience with me, and I will repay you everything." And the lord of that slave felt compassion and released him and forgave him the debt (Matthew 18:23–27).

Matthew here used the strongest word in the Greek language for feelings of compassion, describing an emotion that moves a person to the very depths of his being.[1] William Barker appraised the slave's debt by saying,

> To give some idea of what a colossal debt this was, the total tax income of the five provinces of Palestine . . . was only eight hundred talents. In other words, the servant's debt was over ten times the amount of the national budget.[2]

The parable emphasized that no individual could ever repay such a debt!

A favorite American folksong expresses this sentiment beautifully:

He paid a debt He did not owe,
I owed a debt I could not pay,
I needed someone to wash my sins away.
And now I sing a brand new song, Amazing Grace!
Christ Jesus paid a debt that I could never pay.

God had told Adam that he would die if he disobeyed (Genesis 2:16–17), and God's purpose is unchangeable; it is impossible for Him to lie (Hebrews 6:17–18). There was therefore no human solution to the problem. It required that God come in the flesh and sacrifice His life for the sins of humanity. Jesus, called Immanuel 'God with us', fulfilled that mission (1 Timothy 2:6). Death is the fair wage that sinners deserve, but eternal life in Christ Jesus is God's free gift to man, according to Romans 6:23.

Why must salvation be God's gift?

_____

_____

_____

_____

_____

Discipleship makes demands.

The apostles were a hand-picked group of men who knew the Lord personally, and because of that requirement there can be no apostles today (Acts 1:21–22). We become His disciples by following His teachings, and it was the Lord's command that disciples be made in all nations until the end of days. This is accomplished by teaching people how to be saved, baptizing them into Christ, and nurturing them as Christians (Matthew 28:19–20). They must also be taught that discipleship has demands.

---

1. Debbie Stewart, "It's Greek To Me," in *Christian Woman*, March/April, 2001, 11.
2. Burton Coffman, *Commentary on the Book of Matthew* (Austin: Firm Foundation, 1968), 285.

Jesus said, "If you abide in My word, then you are truly disciples of Mine" (John 8:31). He asked the people, "And why do you call Me, 'Lord, Lord,' and do not do what I say?" (Luke 6:46). John 14:15 teaches that we demonstrate our love for Him by keeping His commandments.

Another time Jesus said, "My sheep hear My voice, and I know them, and they follow Me" (John 10:27). On this passage Phillip Keller comments in his book, *A Shepherd Looks at the Good Shepherd and His Sheep:* "The incredibly beautiful relationship between the Shepherd and His sheep can be and only is possible provided the sheep hear His voice, are known of Him in intimate oneness, and so follow Him in quiet, implicit confidence."[3] Another demand of discipleship is to practice love for others.

Jesus made brotherly love an identifying mark of discipleship (John 13:34–35). The Greek word is *agape*, and Vine says:

> This is not the love of complacency, or affection, that is, it was not drawn out by excellency in its objects. It was an exercise of the Divine will in deliberate choice, made without assignable cause save that which lies in the nature of God Himself.[4]

C. S. Lewis wrote in his book *Mere Christianity* about learning to love those whom we may not even like. He said,

> The rule for all of us is perfectly simple. Do not waste time bothering whether you "love" your neighbor; act as if you did. As soon as we do this we find one of the great secrets. When you are behaving as if you loved someone, you will presently come to love him.[5]

Lewis went on to write that as a boy he suffered from toothaches. While he knew that his mother would give him something to deaden the pain if he asked for it, he also knew that in order to get immediate relief, he would have to agree to pay the price of going to the dentist the next day. It is that way when God takes away the burden of sin from our lives, writes Lewis. He gives wonderful relief but demands something in return by pushing us to a higher level. He puts us into situations where we will have to be very much braver, or more patient, or more loving than we ever dreamed of being before.[6] Discipleship demands that we learn the sometimes difficult task of treating other people the way we ourselves want to be treated (Matthew 7:12).

---

3. Phillip Keller, *A Shepherd Looks at the Good Shepherd* (Grand Rapids: Zondervan, 1978), 171.
4. W. E. Vine, *Dictionary of New Testament Words*, vol. 3, 20-21.
5. C. S. Lewis, *Mere Christianity* (New York: McMillan, 1952), 101.
6. Lewis, *Mere Christianity*, 157.

Disciples must also bear fruit.

Jesus taught this lesson in John 15:8. He pictured Himself as a vine, and He taught that branches which are alive in Him produce fruit. Jesus has the water of life (John 7:37–38) which every healthy tree must have in order to produce fruit (Psalm 1). It is living water, according to John 4:10–14, like that which the Samaritan woman tasted. And like her, when we have drunk of it, we will want to share it with others (Isaiah 12:3).

God looks for evidence of the fruit of the Spirit in our lives—love, joy, peace, patience, kindness, goodness, faithfulness, gentleness, and self-control (Galatians 5:22–23). As long as we remain in Christ, cultivating these virtues, God patiently works with us so we can become even more productive for Him (2 Peter 1:8).

Count the cost before you start.

To the multitudes Jesus said, "If anyone comes to Me, and does not hate his own father and mother and wife and children and brothers and sisters, yes, and even his own life, he cannot be My disciple" (Luke 14:26). This was a hard saying, but it is evident from 1 John 3:15 and Matthew 5:43–44 that He was not speaking about a malicious hatred. Vine says the Greek meaning of *hate* conveys "relative preference of one thing over another." No one can be a true disciple who does not make his service and obedience to Christ more important than even his own life. Paul put it this way: "I have been crucified with Christ; and it is no longer I who live, but Christ lives in me" (Galatians 2:20).

What is indicated by a failure to produce fruit?

Jesus told the story of a man who started to build a tower before calculating the cost; and when he was unable to finish, his neighbors ridiculed him. In another example He cautioned that any king who went into battle without first assessing his chances of victory would be unwise. It is sobering to read that we must renounce all to become His disciple (Luke 14:28–33).

Jesus was not demanding that we take a vow of poverty, as some religious orders do. In fact, Paul admonished that we work with our hands so we can help

What has discipleship cost me?

_____

_____

_____

_____

_____

those in need (Ephesians 4:28). But we must relinquish all claim on our possessions as being our own, realizing that they, along with our very lives, belong to God. Concerning this verse Coffman states, "Every soul that contemplates the terms of discipleship as outlined here must fall upon his knees and say, 'Lord, I am a disciple; help me to be a disciple.'"[7]

---

7. Burton Coffman, *Commentary on Luke* (Austin: Firm Foundation, 1975), 319-320.

Points To Remember

◆ God's gift is unmerited.

◆ Discipleship makes demands.

◆ Disciples must also bear fruit.

◆ Count the cost before you start.

Points To Ponder

◆ *The value of the Bible doesn't consist in merely knowing it, but in obeying it.*

◆ *Duty makes us do things well, but love makes us do them beautifully.*

◆ *"Him who would valiant be 'gainst all disaster, Let him in constancy, follow the Master." John Bunyan*

◆ *"The way to bliss lies not on beds of down, And he that had no cross deserves no crown." Francis Quarles*

12

What Is Truth?

N. B. Hardeman preaching
Ryman Auditorium
Nashville, Tennessee
1922

(Eliza Wade married John B. Hardeman at the age of 19. N. B. was
less than three years old; she was most influential in his upbringing.)

A cafeteria-style approach to religion where every person
may pick and choose what he believes is reminiscent of a time
in Israel when every man did what was right in his own eyes.
God has never left man without a revelation of divine truth.

"I am the way, and the truth, and the life;
no one comes to the Father, but through Me."

John 14:6

Pilate said to Him,

"What is truth?" And when

he had said this, he went out again

to the Jews, and said to them,

"I find no guilt in Him."

John 18:38

What Is Truth?

A Lesson on Truth

John 18:28–40

Jesus: The Way, the Truth, and the Life

The Week of His Passion

Luke records that Jesus appeared to the apostles over a period of forty days after His passion (Acts 1:3). The word *passion* is from a Greek form which means "to suffer," and it has come to represent the last few days of Jesus' life. Some religious groups observe Passion Week, and thousands of visitors travel to Bavaria every ten years to see the celebrated Passion Play which depicts His death.

Jesus' last week is the focal point of the Gospels of Mark and John. Mark devotes approximately forty percent of his account to the Lord's final journey to Jerusalem and the events that surrounded His death. More than one-third of John's narrative involves the last twenty-four hours of His life.[1]

Jesus and the twelve were heading for Jerusalem, accompanied by a large multitude. He had only recently worked a great miracle in raising His friend Lazarus from the dead—His third raising of the dead recorded in the Gospels— and it caused many Jews to believe in Him. When the report reached the Sanhedrin, the Jewish supreme court, its leaders took counsel that very day to put Jesus to death (John 11:53), even though there was no denying that Lazarus, who had been dead for four days, was alive again. Jesus knew what awaited Him in Jerusalem, however, and on the way He took the twelve aside to prepare them. He said:

> Behold, we are going up to Jerusalem, and the Son of Man will be delivered to the chief priests and the scribes; and they will condemn Him to death, and will deliver Him to the Gentiles. And they will mock Him and spit upon Him, and scourge Him, and kill Him, and three days later He will rise again (Mark 10:33–34).

Luke adds that the apostles did not understand any of these things, which became obvious when James and John, along with their mother, requested places of prominence in His kingdom. Their mother was Salome, the wife of Zebedee; and some scholars have suggested, by comparing the Gospel accounts, that she was the sister of Mary mentioned in John 19:25. If that be true, it

---

1. Wayne Jackson, "Examining the Four Gospels," *The Christian Courier*, October 11, 2000, <http://www.christiancourier.com/archives>.

might account for why she accompanied them throughout Galilee and minis-tered to Jesus (Mark 15:40–41). It might also explain her boldness in asking that her sons be favored. It would even shed light on why Jesus entrusted His mother's care to John after His death. We only know, however, that the request stirred up controversy among the twelve.

On the road Jesus healed blind Bartimaeus, who joined in the throng of peo-ple glorifying Him (Luke 18:43). The Lord knew that soon all His followers would desert Him, and He would suffer alone. Nearing Jerusalem, crowds met Him with palm branches and hosannas, fulfilling the prophecy in Zechariah 9:9. As the entourage descended from the Mount of Olives and Jesus caught His first glimpse of the holy city, He was overwhelmed with emotion; He wept (Luke 19:41). He could see the horrible destruction destined for that beautiful and ancient capital because its leaders were about to reject the Messiah whose com-ing they had long anticipated.

It was an emotional week for Jesus. He must have agonized over His impending death, but perhaps He dreaded most being separated from the Father when He took on the sins of mankind. There must have been moments when the anticipation of completing redemption's work thrilled His soul. The writer of Hebrews says that He despised the shame His death would bring, but He endured it for the joy set before Him (Hebrews 12:2). (What a marvelous pas-sage!) That week was indeed a time of intense passion.

Legacy of Truth

The following day Jesus went into the temple and threw out all who bought and sold, which the apostles would later remember as a fulfillment of Psalm 69:9. He spoke boldly to the crowds, and they marveled at His teaching (Mark 11:18). He challenged the Pharisees with parables foretelling His death; and although the leaders realized that He was exposing them, they were afraid to seize Him before the crowds (Mark 12:12). They decided, instead, upon a strat-egy of entrapment and sent their own disciples to question Him. "And they came and said to Him, 'Teacher, we know that You are truthful, and defer to no one; for You are not partial to any, but teach the way of God in truth. Is it law-ful to pay a poll-tax to Caesar, or not?'"

Jesus detected their intent at once and answered, "Why are you testing me, you hypocrites?"(Mark 12:15). Examining a coin, He instructed them to render to Caesar the things that belonged to him and to God the things that were God's. Once again, they marveled at His ability to anticipate them.

He said to them:

> Woe to you, scribes and Pharisees, hypocrites! For you clean the outside of the cup and of the dish, but inside they are full of robbery and self-indulgence . . . You are like whitewashed tombs which on the outside appear beautiful, but inside they are full of dead men's bones and all uncleanness (Matthew 23:25–27).

It was a fitting description of men about to deliver the Son of God to be crucified, but afraid to enter Pilate's hall lest they be defiled (John 18:28). According to John, some of these very rulers believed in Jesus but would not confess Him lest they be ostracized from the synagogue (John 12:42). Ironically, the Pharisees—from the Aramaic meaning "separate"—were dedicated to upholding the truth. In reality, they were determined to kill the One who brought words of truth from God Himself (John 8:40).

Night with Ebon Pinion

Throughout that week, the apostles became increasingly apprehensive and fearful. Peter, often overconfident, declared that he would not forsake Jesus if all others should (Matthew 26:33). But Jesus told him, "Simon, Simon, behold, Satan has demanded permission to sift you like wheat; but I have prayed for you, that your faith may not fail; and you, when once you have turned again, strengthen your brothers" (Luke 22:31–32).

Two days before the Passover, Satan, who was crouched at the door, found an entrance into the heart of Judas Iscariot, and that apostle sought an opportunity to betray Jesus into the hands of His enemies (Luke 22:3–6). The Scripture does not say exactly what motivated him. It may have been pure greed or personal ambition or even politics. Perhaps he feared for his own life. But he agreed to deliver Jesus to His enemies for thirty pieces of silver, the price of a slave (Exodus 21:32).

With the Passover drawing near, Jesus observed it with the twelve and instituted the Lord's supper, telling them that He was going to die. Judas, who may have been carrying the blood-money on him, dined with the group and allowed the Savior to bathe his feet before Jesus said to him, "What you do, do quickly" (John 13:27).

After Judas' departure, Jesus began to console the apostles, promising to send them the Spirit of truth to abide with them in the days ahead (John 14:16–17). But when supper was ended and they had sung a hymn, Jesus made His way to Gethsemane, the garden where He often prayed; and the disciples followed Him. It was to be a night of *ebon pinion* 'dark passion', in the words of L. H. Jameson.

Judas also knew the spot, and it was there that he led a band of soldiers and officers bearing torches and weapons. The soldiers arrested and bound Jesus and carried Him first to Annas and then to Caiaphas, the high priest (John 18:13, 24). Throughout that terrible night, Jesus was mocked and beaten; and when morning arrived, they tied Him up and led Him to the palace of their governor, Pontius Pilate.

The Jews presented Pilate with three specific charges concerning Jesus. He was perverting the nation, forbidding men to pay tribute to Caesar, and claiming to be the Christ. When Pilate asked, "Are you the King of the Jews?" Jesus replied, "Are you saying this on your own initiative, or did others tell you about Me?"

"I am not a Jew, am I?" Pilate retorted. "Your own nation and the chief priests delivered You up to me; what have You done?"

Jesus answered, "My kingdom is not of this world. If My kingdom were of this world, then My servants would be fighting, that I might not be delivered up to the Jews; but as it is, My kingdom is not of this realm" (John 18:36).

The Final Question

Pilate then queried, "So You are a king?" Jesus answered, "You say correctly that I am a king. For this I have been born, and for this I have come into the world, to bear witness to the truth. Everyone who is of the truth hears My voice."

Had Jesus spoken of power or wealth, Pilate might have shown more interest. As it was, hearing that Jesus' mission was to proclaim the truth, he dismissed Him with a cynical question: "What is truth?" By his own admission he could find no guilt in Jesus, yet he delivered Him to His enemies to be crucified, knowing that His treatment was a mockery of justice and a complete disregard of civil law.

Considerable controversy concerning the propriety of the trial of Jesus has existed ever since His crucifixion. Volumes have been searched in an effort to find some legal justification for the verdict rendered, but nowhere is there to be found any logical or legal excuse for the absolute disregard of the then existing Hebrew code, nor the customs usually followed in criminal proceedings before Jewish courts.[2]

---

2. Robert Boyd, "The (Mis)Trial of Jesus," *World's Bible Handbook* (Iowa Falls: World Bible Publishers, 1991), 458-459.

Can I really know and understand the truth?

All truth originates with God.

Psalm 117 has the distinction of being the shortest chapter, as well as the middle chapter, in the entire Bible. It says, "Praise the Lord, all nations; laud Him all peoples! For His lovingkindness is great toward us, and the truth of the Lord is everlasting, Praise the Lord!" This psalm serves as the basis of a well-known hymn.

Throughout Psalm 119, this the longest of the psalms, the author repeatedly extols the truth of God's Word. He writes, "Do not take the word of truth utterly out of my mouth" (119:43). "Thy law is truth" he says (v. 142), and "all Thy commandments are truth" (v. 151).

Another passage reads, "For Thy lovingkindness is great above the heavens; and Thy truth reaches to the skies" (Psalm 108:4). Psalm 85:10 declares that "lovingkindness and truth have met together; righteousness and peace have kissed each other." Certainly that occurred when Jesus died on the cross.

What is the only reliable source of truth known to man? (Romans 3:4)

_____

_____

_____

_____

_____

John wrote of the incarnate Word saying, "We beheld His glory, glory as of the only begotten from the Father, full of grace and truth" (John 1:14). Three of the major world religions—Hinduism, Buddhism, and Confucianism—were already in existence by the time Jesus came. (Islam would not develop until some six hundred years later.) Jesus did not hesitate to declare, "I am the way, and the truth, and the life; no one comes to the Father, but through Me" (John 14:6). According to Hebrews 1:1–2, God has never left man without a revelation of divine truth.

Truth can be determined.

Solomon advises that if you incline your ear to God's words and trust in Him, you can "know the certainty of the words of truth," and you will be able to correctly answer the one who sends unto you (Proverbs 22:21; compare 1 Peter 3:15). The apostle John did not just acknowledge that truth existed; He wrote to brethren who knew the truth (1 John 2:21; 2 John 1). Truth can be understood! Jesus Himself promised that "you shall know the truth, and the truth shall make you free" (John 8:32). Since Satan is a liar (John 8:44), it is no wonder that he continues to do everything within his power to convince the world that truth is unattainable.

If truth cannot be determined, can anything be condemned?

Truth is absolute and eternal.

It is not popular in our day to believe in absolute truth. In fact, statistics indicate that seventy percent of Americans now believe there is no such thing as absolute truth.[3] We are living in the age of *Post-modernism* which, according to one writer, has impacted "our literature, our dress, our art, our architecture, our music, our sense of right and wrong, our self-identity, and our theology."[4] How did we get to this point?

By the beginning of the second century, a complete canon of New Testament Scripture existed. But gradually, the Christian world slipped into a period of apostasy as the Scriptures were withheld from the common people by powerful religious leaders. Ignorance of the truth ushered in the period called the *Dark Ages.*

As people began to demand the right to think for themselves, a great reformation occurred. Individuals realized that the truth could be deduced through principles of logic and reasoning. With the invention of the printing press, the Word of God found its way into the hands of many ordinary people. Most of them viewed the Bible as the universal authority in matters of faith and reason. Their new-found freedom to think independently created an explosion of learning. The thirst for knowledge and truth also led to great scientific discovery.

3. Phil Sanders, *Adrift* (Nashville: Gospel Advocate, 2000), 26.
4. Sanders, class lecture at Nashville School of Preaching and Biblical Studies, 2000.

Darwin's ideas on evolution, a theory by his own admission, were taken by some as proof that empirical science is the most reliable source of knowledge.[5] A new period, referred to as the *Age of Modernism*, began in the 1700s.

It was an era of exciting discovery and invention. Men began to elevate science above God's written revelation, while still paying lip-service to religious teachings. Since the 1970s, however, a virtual explosion of modern technology has ushered in the present period of *Postmodernism*. The ideas of postmodernists have greatly impacted our views on religion and the nature of truth. These trends are detailed in Phil Sanders' excellent book, *Adrift*.

One suggestion of postmodernists is that we need a non-doctrinal type of Christianity in today's world. Long-cherished teachings are no longer believed by many who claim to be Christians. One writer has commented, "We are a religious people, but inwardly our religious beliefs make no difference in how we live."[6]

Another trend is the cafeteria-style approach to religion where every person may pick-and-choose what he believes. It is reminiscent of a time in Israel when every man did what was right in his own eyes (Judges 17:6). We are taught that everyone's affirmation of faith is equally valid: "I'm okay, you're okay." The people described in 2 Kings 17:41 feared God but also served their idols, and many in our own culture feel right at home with that practice. They agree with the Athenians that we should honor every religious persuasion of men (Acts 17:23).

Postmodernists view all truth as relative. The situation, not an absolute standard, determines what is right and what is wrong. The late Batsell Baxter, in his book, *I Believe Because*, tells of addressing a class of students at a large state university some years ago in which he posed the question, "Is truth relative?" He reported that within that class he was unable to establish a single moral, ethical principle which the group would accept as wrong under any circumstances.[7]

The Greek mathematician Archimedes once said, "Give me a place to stand and I will move the earth."[8] Postmodernism is removing the foundations of our society, leaving us to ask along with the psalmist: "If the foundations are destroyed, what can the righteous do?" (Psalm 11:3). We can take assurance in

---

5. Sanders, quoting Phillip E. Johnson, *Darwin on Trial.*
6. Charles Colson, *Kingdoms in Conflict* (Grand Rapids: Zondervan, 1987), 214.
7. Batsell Barrett Baxter, *I Believe Because* (Grand Rapids: Baker, 1976), 235-236.
8. Batsell Barrett Baxter, *America* (Grand Rapids: Baker, 1974), 9.

the promise that God's word is "settled in heaven" (Psalm 119:89), and that even when it is attacked, it will rise again.

> Truth, crushed to earth, shall rise again;
> Th' eternal years of God are hers;
> But Error, wounded, writhes in pain,
> And dies among his worshipers.[9]

The truth can set men free.

When I taught school, we studied the American constitution and noted that our forefathers appealed to a body of truths which they considered to be self-evident: "that all men are created equal, that they are endowed by their Creator with certain unalienable Rights, that among these are Life, Liberty and the pursuit of Happiness." As we memorized these meaningful lines and talked

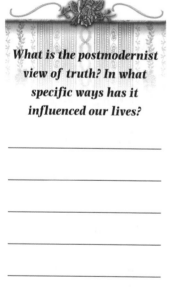

What is the postmodernist view of truth? In what specific ways has it influenced our lives?

about rights versus responsibility, I sometimes asked the students if they would like to live in a world where everyone had the right to do whatever he wanted. Of course, most of them thought it would be great. But as we considered that freedom from all rules would mean the end of anyone's personal rights and protection, and we discussed the implications of it, even those fifth graders could see that we can't have it both ways.

The atheist Julian Huxley once commented that somehow or other "man functions better if he acts as though God is there." Where there are no moral absolutes, Darwin's "survival of the fittest" becomes the law. Television shows like "Survivor" give us food for thought. How many of us would want to live in a world where the quest to become number one was the motivating thought of everyone? The new-found freedom of this generation has resulted in a soaring crime rate, declining morals, alcohol and drug abuse, and a sub-standard work ethic. We have freed ourselves from many things that made us great as a nation. It has led one analyst to say, "This whole emphasis today on the individual doing what he thinks

---

9. William Cullen Bryant, "The Battle-Field," stanza 9, in *The Poetical Works of William Cullen Bryant* (1837), 276.

is right can only lead to moral anarchy . . . A society can't exist that is chaotic."[10]

Real freedom, according to Jesus, is found in embracing the truth which is eternal (John 8:32). However maligned, truth will not die. We are reminded of James Russell Lowell's allusion:

Truth forever on the scaffold,
Wrong forever on the throne—
Yet that scaffold sways the future,
And, behind the dim unknown
Standeth God within the shadow,
Keeping watch above his own.[11]

Points To Remember

◆ All truth originates from God.

◆ Truth can be determined.

◆ Truth is absolute and eternal.

◆ The truth can set men free.

Points To Ponder

◆ *"The supply of truth always exceeds the demand." Josh Billings*

◆ *"Hell is truth seen too late—duty neglected in its season." Tryon Edwards*

◆ *We admire the truth, provided it agrees with our views.*

◆ *Truth often hurts, but it's the lie that leaves the scars.*

---

10. Baxter, *America*, 121.
11. James Russell Lowell, "The Present Crisis," stanza 8.

~ 13 ~

What Then Shall I Do with Jesus?

T. B. Larimore baptizing my grandfather,
Robert Hedge Porch
Bakerville, Tennessee
c. 1909

All the armies that ever marched and all the navies that were ever built and all the kings that ever reigned, put together, have not affected the life of man upon this earth, as much as the One Solitary Life.

"I believe that Jesus Christ is the Son of God . . .
and they both went down into the water,
Phillip as well as the eunuch, and he baptized him."

Acts 8:37–38

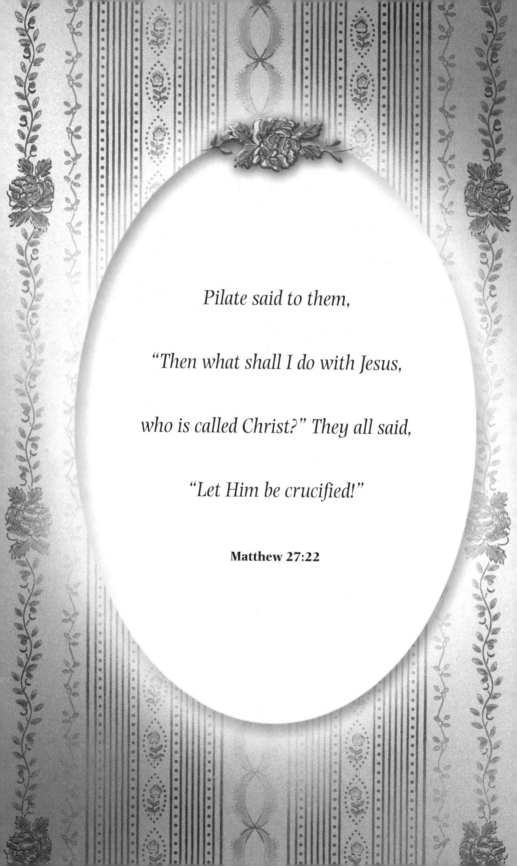

Pilate said to them,

"Then what shall I do with Jesus,

who is called Christ?" They all said,

"Let Him be crucified!"

Matthew 27:22

What Then Shall I Do with Jesus?

A Lesson on Salvation

Matthew 27:11–22

Redemption's Work Completed

"I Find No Crime in Him."

During the trial of Jesus, Pilate learned that his prisoner was a Galilean and decided to send Him to Herod, the tetrarch of Galilee, who was in Jerusalem. Herod was delighted to see Jesus, for he had heard about Him and had long hoped to see Him work a miracle. He was likely disappointed that he got no performance; he sent Him back to Pilate. Since neither official could find any fault in Him, Pilate was of a mind to scourge Jesus and release Him.

The scourging itself was a horrible punishment that could result in death. It involved being stripped to the waist and bound in a stooping position to a post. The Jews' law forbade giving more than forty stripes, but the Romans were not bound by it and were known to beat an individual to death on occasion. The scourge was a leather thong containing knots and small pieces of bone or lead, and it often turned the victim into an unrecognizable mass of bleeding flesh.

Pilate knew the rulers had delivered Jesus out of envy (Matthew 27:18). He reminded them that since he customarily released a prisoner during Passover, he could pardon Jesus; but the multitude, at the instigation of the leaders, began chanting for the release of Barabbas, an insurrectionist and murderer.

Pilate's wife sent him word saying, "Have nothing to do with that righteous Man; for last night I suffered greatly in a dream because of Him" (Matthew 27:19). To make matters worse, the Jews revealed that they believed Jesus deserved to die because He claimed to be the Son of God (John 19:7). This frightened Pilate, and he took Jesus inside the Praetorium to question Him further. He wanted Jesus to confirm who He was and said to Him, "Do you not know that I have authority to release you, and I have authority to crucify you?" (John 19:10). Jesus told him plainly, "You would have no authority over Me, unless it had been given you from above" (v. 11).

What to do with Jesus—that was Pilate's dilemma. The man was innocent, quite possibly divine, he thought. Yet the people were insistent, even threatening his good favor with Caesar should he release Him (John 19:12). When he saw that a riot was underway, he called for water to wash his hands and said, "I am innocent of this Man's blood; see to that yourselves" (Matthew 27:24).

"It is finished."

Around nine o'clock soldiers led Jesus to the place called Golgotha, that is, "the place of a skull" (Matthew 27:33; Mark 15:25). No doubt He was bruised and bleeding profusely from the scourging and from scalp wounds inflicted by a crown of thorns soldiers had roughly thrust upon His head. One physician has cataloged five specific types of wounds He received that day: contusions from being beaten (Micah 5:1; Matthew 27:30; John 18:22); lacerations from the scourging (Psalm 129:3; Isaiah 50:6; Matthew 27:26); penetrations from the crown of thorns (Matthew 27:29); perforations from the nails in His hands and feet (John 20:25); and an incision made by a Roman soldier's spear (Zechariah 12:10; John 19:34). It was customary for the condemned to carry his own crossbeam to the place of execution, where the victim would be nailed or tied to it and hoisted upon a stationary support. Jesus was unable to bear the weight of the cross in His weakened condition, so one from the crowd, Simon, a man of Cyrene, carried it for Him. Perhaps, as they led Him outside the city, Jesus thought about Isaiah's vision of a lamb being led to slaughter (Isaiah 53:7).[1]

Under Moses' law, the sins of the people required that two male goats be brought before the High Priest on the yearly Day of Atonement. One he slew as an offering, sprinkling its blood within the Most Holy Place (Leviticus 16:5, 15). Its body had to be taken outside the camp, however, which made those who bore it unclean (Leviticus 16:27–28). The scapegoat he sent into the wilderness, having laid upon it the sins of the people (Leviticus 16:10, 21–22). Was Jesus thinking of this rich symbolism as they led Him out?

Other nations had practiced crucifixion for hundreds of years, but it was a favorite means of execution among the Romans. According to history, beginning in A.D. 66 they crucified so many Jews that the executioners ran out of wood for crosses! It was a horrible death; the victim might endure for several agonizing days. Spikes were driven between the bones just above the wrist. The legs were pressed together and twisted to one side, with a large spike driven through the heel and into the wood. A small piece of wood called a *sedecula* provided a support shelf on which the victim halfway sat.

In 1970 archaeologists found the first remains ever discovered of a crucified man, about two thousand years old. It revealed a grisly tale. The spike that pierced his heel bones had struck a knot in the wood and become imbedded in

---

1. Robert Boyd, *World's Bible Handbook* (Iowa Falls: World Bible Publishers, Inc., 1991), 463-465.

the cross. As a result, at his burial someone cut off his feet above the ankles, and those amputated, still pierced feet, were buried with the remains.[2]

They crucified Jesus between two thieves and beneath an inscription written in three languages that identified Him as the "King of the Jews." Their leaders objected, but Pilate refused to remove the sign in what might have been a parting shot at those who had caused Him such aggravation. Soldiers divided His garments but cast lots for His robe, fulfilling Psalm 22:18. Passersby taunted Him and laughed saying, "Save yourself, and come down from the cross!" (Mark 15:30).

Some women in the crowd were weeping for Jesus (Luke 23:27–29), while the chief priests and the soldiers mocked Him (vv. 35–36). One of the thieves also railed on Him, but the other believed, according to Luke. A few friends and relatives stood near the cross, close enough to hear the words He uttered (John 19:25). And Luke records that "the people stood by, looking on" (Luke 23:35). It leads me to wonder, had I been present, where I would have stood. Where might you have been?

The sky grew black, and from noon until three o'clock there was darkness over the land. Tetullian, writing around A.D. 200, made mention of the darkness and wrote that some "who did not know the prophecy" thought it an eclipse.[3] The duration, however, was too long; and the timing made that impossible, since the Passover always fell during a full moon, when no eclipse could occur.

Jesus spoke but seven times during the six hours He hanged there, once to ask John to care for His mother. Luke also records that during the crucifixion He was saying, "Father, forgive them; for they do not know what they are doing" (Luke 23:34). The verb tense, which is imperfect, implies that He said it repeatedly. Near three o'clock, as the evening sacrifice was being offered in the temple, Jesus cried out with a loud voice, "My God, My God, why hast Thou forsaken Me?" (Matthew 27:46). Then John records:

> After this, Jesus, knowing that all things had already been accomplished, in order that the Scripture might be fulfilled, said, "I am thirsty." A jar full of sour wine was standing there; so they put a sponge full of the sour wine upon a branch of hyssop, and brought it up to His mouth. When Jesus therefore had received the sour wine, He said, "It is finished!" And He bowed His head and gave up His spirit (John 19:28–30).

---

2. Boyd, *Bible Handbook*, 389.
3. Burton Coffman, *Commentary on Matthew* (Austin, TX: Firm Foundation, 1968), 484–485.

No doubt the pangs of thirst were upon Jesus, but He also knew the prophecy of Psalm 69:21. Even in agony He was conscious of the need to fulfill every Scripture and to finish the mission envisioned before the ages.

In the temple, the veil was torn in two from top to bottom. The earth began to quake, rocks were split, and tombs were opened (Matthew 27:51–52). As the centurion and the other guards at the cross saw the things that were happening, they were frightened and confessed, "Truly, this was the Son of God!" (v. 54).

"He Has Risen."

The Sabbath, which began at 6:00 P.M., was rapidly approaching; and the leaders hurried to remove the bodies in accordance with the Scripture (Deuteronomy 21:23). The soldiers were surprised to find Jesus already dead and did not break His legs as they did the others. (Breaking the legs prevented the victim from supporting himself and led to suffocation.) Thus they fulfilled the prophecy that not a bone of Him would be broken (Psalm 34:20).

Jesus' body was hastily removed and placed in the new tomb of a man named Joseph, a rich disciple from Arimathea (Matthew 27:57–60). They bound it in linen with a generous amount of spices, then rolled a great stone before the door. Knowing Jesus' promise that He would rise the third day, the rulers requested and received a guard to seal the tomb and watch it, lest His disciples steal the body and claim that He had risen from the dead.

Early on the first day of the week, before sunrise, a group of women—including Mary Magdalene, Mary the mother of James, Salome, and Joanna—set out for the garden (Mark 16:1; Luke 24:10). On the way, they discussed among themselves whom they would get to roll back the heavy stone. To their surprise, they found the stone already moved, and looking inside they saw that the body was gone.

While they stood perplexed, two men in dazzling white appeared, and one of them said, "Do not be afraid; for I know that you are looking for Jesus who has been crucified. He is not here, for He has risen, just as He said. Come, see the place where He was lying" (Matthew 28:5–6). The women were filled with fear and amazement to the point that they trembled, but they hurried away with great joy to bring word to the disciples (Matthew 28:8).

Matthew records the occurrence of an earthquake early that morning as an angel from Heaven descended, rolled away the stone, and sat upon it. His appearance as lightning so terrified the guards that they shook and became as dead men (Matthew 28:4). Evidently, the arrival of the women sent some of them fleeing into the city where they reported to the chief priests, whose worst fears were realized with the body of Jesus missing and their own guards now able to testify to His resurrection. The priests, therefore, took counsel with the elders and gave a large sum of money to those men to lie. The story they concocted was ludicrous, for they could only claim that while the whole guard slept, Jesus' disciples had broken the seal, moved the massive stone—which would have caused quite a commotion—and stolen His body (Matthew 28:12–13). (Later, a large number of the priests were obedient to the faith, according to Acts 6:7. They must have found this act shameful.)

"I Have Seen the Lord."

Mary Magdalene hurried to find Peter and John, who ran to see for themselves if what she told them was true. John, the swifter of the two, arrived first; and stooping down, he looked inside but saw no body. He did observe the way in which the linen wrappings were laying there, and Peter, who went in, also noted the position of the grave clothes and the face-cloth rolled up by itself. John later testified that the sight caused him to believe.

The two left, but Mary remained outside weeping. She asked someone whom she supposed to be the gardener, "Sir, if you have carried Him away, tell me where you have laid Him, and I will take Him away." We can only guess how Mary would have accomplished that, but she would have tried. It must have been with great tenderness that Jesus said to her, "Mary!" When she saw it was Jesus, she was overwhelmed and replied, "Master!" She took hold of His feet and worshiped (Matthew 28:9), for He said to her gently, "Stop clinging to Me, for I have not yet ascended to the Father" (John 20:17).

Jesus sent her back to tell the others who were grieving, but they did not believe her (Mark 16:11). How like the Master to appear first to this devoted woman from whom He had cast out demons, the one who had gratefully ministered to Him out of her private means (Luke 8:1–3), followed Him to the cross, set out before daylight to tend His dead body, and now remained by His tomb weeping when all others had fled. Mary was a faithful disciple, doing what she could in her quiet way. We are reminded of Jesus' saying in Matthew 7:8 that the one who seeks, finds.

Later in the day Jesus appeared in another form to two disciples as they traveled from the city to Emmaus, a village seven miles distant. He inquired of them about the events of the weekend, and they told Him sadly about the death of the one they considered a prophet mighty in deed and word, whom they had hoped would be the one to redeem Israel. Furthermore, they were perplexed that some of their women, who had gone early to the tomb, had seen a vision of angels who claimed that He was alive. Then Jesus began at Moses and the prophets and explained to them "the things concerning Himself in all the Scriptures." As they stopped and prepared to share a meal, Jesus blessed the bread; and their eyes were opened. Just as they recognized Him, He vanished from their sight (Luke 24:13–31).

These men hurried back to Jerusalem and told the disciples what had happened. Later, as they met behind closed doors, Jesus appeared in their midst and invited them to inspect the imprints of the nails in His hands and feet. He assured them that He was not a spirit, for no ghost has flesh and bones as He had. He even ate food, which filled them with joy and wonder.

But Thomas, who was not present, could not believe their report. The following week Jesus appeared again, and this time He invited Thomas to feel the hole in His side. The sight of that wounded body led Thomas to exclaim, "My Lord and my God" (John 20:28).

"You Are Witnesses of These Things."

Over a period of forty days the Lord appeared to His disciples several times, even joining them in Galilee. Luke records that He "opens their minds to understand the Scriptures" (Luke 24:45). And He told them:

> Thus it is written, that the Christ should suffer and rise again from the dead the third day; and that repentance for forgiveness of sins should be proclaimed in His name to all the nations, beginning from Jerusalem. You are witnesses of these things. And behold, I am sending forth the promise of My Father upon you; but you are to stay in the city until you are clothed with power from on high (Luke 24:46–49).

He gave them a great commission, saying, "Go into all the world and preach the gospel to every creature. He who believes and is immersed shall be saved, but he who does not believe shall be condemned" (Mark 16:15–16 McCORD).

Ten days before Pentecost, He led them to the Mount of Olives where He renewed His promise, saying, "You shall receive power when the Holy Spirit has come upon you; and you shall be My witnesses both in Jerusalem, and in all Judea and Samaria, and even to the remotest part of the earth" (Acts 1:8). After Jesus said these things, He was lifted up into the clouds. Two men in white clothing appeared beside them with the assurance that Jesus would come again as they had seen Him go into Heaven.

The apostles returned to Jerusalem to await the power, and in the days that followed they prayed for guidance in selecting a twelfth apostle, Matthias, to take the place of Judas who had killed himself. A group of about 120—including the women and Mary, His mother, along with His own brothers, now themselves believers—were continually devoting themselves to prayer (John 7:5; Acts 1:14).

When the day of Pentecost arrived, the sound as a violent, rushing wind filled their house and tongues as of fire rested upon the twelve apostles, and they were filled with the Holy Spirit. They began to speak the mighty deeds of God in other languages, so that all those assembled in Jerusalem could hear the message in their own tongues. (Luke lists some fifteen nationalities present.) Peter stood and preached powerfully, appealing to the Old Testament prophets and telling those assembled:

> This Man, delivered up by the predetermined plan and foreknowledge of God, you nailed to a cross by the hands of godless men and put Him to death. And God raised Him up again, putting an end to the agony of death, since it was impossible for Him to be held in its power (Acts 2:23–24).

He testified, "This Jesus God raised up again, to which we are all witnesses" (Acts 2:32) and concluded, "Let all the house of Israel know for certain that God has made Him both Lord and Christ—this Jesus whom you crucified" (Acts 2:36). Luke records that the people were "pierced to the heart." No doubt, many were already convinced that an innocent man had been put to death. Peter's sermon, coupled with the missing body—for which the authorities could not account—opened their eyes so that they believed. They cried out, "Men, brothers, what should we do?" (Acts 2:37 McCORD).

Must I, too, deal with Jesus?

Question: "What shall [I] do?" (Acts 2:37).

The Holy Spirit had convicted those assembled on Pentecost of their sin. Some translations read that they were "cut" or "pierced" to the heart. McCord says "stabbed in their heart," and Vine indicates the verb means "to strike or prick violently, to stun" and "is used of strong emotion." They were convinced that Jesus was Lord and Christ; they knew it with certainty as believers (Acts 2:36, 44).

Peter answered their question, telling them, "Change your hearts, and let each one of you be immersed in the name of Jesus Christ, so that your sins might be forgiven, and you shall receive the gift of the Holy Spirit" (Acts 2:38 McCORD). Other translations use the word *repent*, which signifies a change of mind or purpose for the better, according to Vine.[4] Their new purpose involved a change of allegiance, for Peter told them to be baptized in the name of Jesus Christ. Vine says that the baptized person was closely bound to, and became the property of, the one into whose name he was baptized.[5] The Greek *baptizo* always means to immerse, therefore Paul later wrote that we are baptized into Christ's death, being buried with Him through baptism into death, adding that "if we have become united with Him in the likeness of His death, certainly we shall be also in the likeness of His resurrection" (Romans 6:3–5). As a result, those who accepted the message were immersed, and God added converts to their number daily (Acts 2:47).

Question: "What prevents me from being baptized?"

There can be no doubt that those saved on Pentecost and added to the fellowship of the disciples made up the nucleus of the early church. (See Acts 8:2.) They called themselves believers (2:44) before the name Christian became common. (See Acts 2:44; 11:26.) The book of Acts records the beginning and growth of the church as it spread from Jerusalem into Judea and Samaria and eventually into more remote areas of the earth (Acts 1:8). With the rise of persecution, believers scattered everywhere "preaching the word" (Acts 8:4).

There are seven chapters in the book of Acts in which examples of conversion are discussed. They are Acts 2, 8, 9, 10, 11, 16, and 18. In each case, individuals obeyed the same gospel message Peter preached in Acts 2. One example is that of an Ethiopian eunuch whom Philip taught in Acts 8:35–39.

This man, a court official connected to the queen of Ethiopia, had been in Jerusalem to worship, where he likely heard about Jesus of Nazareth and observed that thousands had accepted Him as Lord. It must have greatly stirred his interest, for as he returned home he was studying Isaiah's prophecy of the

---

4. W. E. Vine, *Dictionary of New Testament Words*, vol. 3, 280.
5. Ibid., 210.

lamb led to slaughter. Philip, sent by the Holy Spirit to join him, began at the same Scripture and preached Jesus (Acts 8:35). Undoubtedly he told the eunuch about his need to be baptized, because as they approached water, the eunuch said eagerly, "Look! Water! What prevents me from being baptized?" (Acts 8:36).

Upon his confession of Jesus as the Son of God, the eunuch ordered the chariot to stop, and both of them went down into the water, where Philip baptized the man. After he came up out of the water, the eunuch went on his way rejoicing, for he now understood God's great plan which had formerly been to him a mystery. Every other conversion found in Acts, like that of the eunuch, also resulted in an individual's putting on Christ in baptism (Galatians 3:27).

Question: "And now why do [I] delay?" (Acts 22:16).

Next to the Lord Himself, no individual is more prominent in the Scriptures than the apostle Paul, who wrote two-thirds of the New Testament. Paul was a young man who went by the name of Saul when we first encounter him in Acts 7:58. There he was in hearty agreement with those who were stoning to death the first Christian martyr, Stephen. Born a Roman citizen, Saul was a strict Pharisee from a family of Pharisees. He had been educated under Gamaliel, an eminent lawyer, and was a member of the Jewish council. Furthermore, he persecuted Christians with great zeal. Saul was the most unlikely convert to Christianity we can imagine.

As he traveled to Damascus to arrest believers in Christ, he had a vision from Jesus, who said to him, "Saul, Saul, why are you persecuting me?" (Acts 9:4). He was instructed to go into the city where he would be told things that he must do (v. 6). He obeyed; but unlike the eunuch, Saul did not go on his way rejoicing. He was not yet saved although he had obeyed Jesus in all he had been told to do to that point (Acts 26:19). For three days he fasted and prayed (Acts 9:9–11), but he was still unsaved. Then the Lord sent a messenger to him to ask, "And now why do you delay? Arise, and be baptized, and wash away your sins, calling on His name" (Acts 22:16). Saul obeyed that command; he was a chosen vessel, preaching the gospel to the Gentile nations.

Concerning Paul, one has written:

> If ever there was a man in the first century who knew all the arguments against the resurrection of Christ which the Sanhedrin could draw up, that man was Saul of Tarsus. Yet, in spite of all this, he came to believe that Christ had been raised from the dead by the power of God, and, believing this, he became the great apostle Paul who preached the resurrection of Christ throughout the Roman Empire.[6]

Paul was later beheaded in Rome for his defense of the gospel.

Question: "Then what shall I do with Jesus who is called Christ?" (Matthew 27:22).

Pilate had to make a decision about what to do with Jesus. He went against his own conscience and crucified the Son of God. Those who heard the gospel on Pentecost also had a decision to make. Some of them might have formerly been among those shouting, "Crucify Him!" Many opened their hearts to the truth, and in their obedience found forgiveness for all their past sins. The eunuch was eagerly searching for the truth when he found it and obeyed. Perhaps none made so dramatic a turn-around as Paul, who gave up everything for the surpassing value of knowing Christ Jesus as Lord (Philippians 3:8).

Tradition says that each of the apostles, save John, died a horrible martyr's death. They would not have paid that price for a gospel they knew to be false nor would they have followed a person who was simply a good man. The elderly Polycarp was one of many who suffered execution for the name of Jesus in the decades that followed. When the authorities promised to spare him if he would revile the name of Christ, Polycarp replied, "Eighty and six years have I served Him, and He never did me wrong; and how can I now blaspheme my King that has saved me?"[7]

C. S. Lewis wrote of Jesus:

> I am trying here to prevent anyone saying the really foolish thing that people often say about Him: "I'm ready to accept Jesus as a great moral teacher, but I don't accept his claim to be God." You must make your choice. Either this man was, and is, the Son of God; or else a madman or something worse. You can shut him up for a fool, you can spit at him and kill him as a demon, or you can fall at his feet and call him Lord and God. But let us not come away with any patronizing nonsense about his being a great human teacher. He has not left that open to us. He did not intend to.[8]

---

6. Batsell Barrett Baxter, *I Believe Because* (Grand Rapids: Baker, 1976), 229.
7. Isaac Boyle, *The Ecclesiastical History of Eusebius Pamphilus* (Grand Rapids: Baker, 1979), 146.
8. C. S. Lewis, *Mere Christianity* (New York: Macmillan, 1952), 40-41.

God created man knowing the power of sin to bring about his fall. But "God so loved the world" that He purposed beforehand to redeem fallen mankind with the precious blood of a Savior. What matchless love! Throughout the centuries untold numbers of people have sacrificed their possessions, their freedom, and even their very lives for the privilege of serving the Christ. The question for me, and the question for you, now becomes: "What then shall *I* do with Jesus?"

Points To Remember

- ◆ "What shall [I] do?" (Acts 2:37).
- ◆ "What prevents me from being baptized?" (Acts 8:36).
- ◆ "And now why do [I] delay?" (Acts 22:16).
- ◆ "Then what shall I do with Jesus, who is called Christ?" (Matthew 27:22).

Points To Ponder

One Solitary Life

Here is a man who was born in an obscure village, the child of a peasant woman. He worked in a carpenter shop until he was thirty, and then for three years He was an itinerant preacher. He never held an office. He never owned a home. He never wrote a book. He never had a family. He never went to college. He never put his foot inside a big city. He never traveled two hundred miles from the place where he was born. He never did one of the things which usually accompany greatness. He had no credentials but himself.

While he was a young man, the tide of public opinion turned against him. His friends ran away. He was turned over to his enemies. He went through the mockery of a trial. He was nailed to a cross between two thieves. While He was dying, his executioners gambled for the only piece of property he had on earth, and that was his coat. When he was dead, He was laid in a private grave through the pity of a friend.

Nineteen wide centuries have come and gone, and today he is the central figure of the human race and the leader of the column of progress.

I am far within the mark when I say that all the armies that ever marched, and all the navies that were ever built, and all the parliaments that ever sat, and all the kings that ever reigned, put together, have not affected the life of man upon this earth, as the One Solitary Life.

—Anonymous[9]

---

9. Suzy Platt, *Respectfully Quoted: A Dictionary of Quotations*, original source unknown, attributed to James Allan Fancis (1864-1928) (New York: Barnes & Noble, 1993), 175-176.